Appraisal of Investment Projects by

DISCOUNTED CASH FLOW

PRINCIPLES and
SOME SHORT CUT TECHNIQUES

by A. M. ALFRED and J. B. EVANS

Third Edition

CHAPMAN AND HALL

DISCOUNTED CASH FLOW

Appraisal of Investment Projects by

DISCOUNTED CASH FLOW

PRINCIPLES and
SOME SHORT CUT TECHNIQUES

Third Edition

by A. M. ALFRED, B.Sc., B.Sc.(Econ.), A.R.C.S., F.I.S.
and J. B. EVANS, B.A., A.C.I.S.

CHAPMAN AND HALL LTD

11 NEW FETTER LANE LONDON EC4

First published 1965
by Chapman and Hall Ltd,
11 New Fetter Lane, London EC4P 4EE
Reprinted once
Second edition 1967
Reprinted three times
Third edition 1971

Printed in Great Britain by
Latimer Trend & Co. Ltd., Whitstable

SBN 412 10680 9

Distributed in the U.S.A.
by Barnes and Noble, Inc.

Investment Grants

The methods described in this book are not affected by any changes
in investment grants, since they allow the incorporation of any rate
of grant without difficulty.

FOREWORD TO FIRST EDITION

by A. W. Knight, Finance Director, Courtaulds Ltd.

This manual was prepared for use by those in Courtaulds who are concerned in making the financial appraisals which are required when investment decisions are being taken. We began in 1961 to study the suitability for our purposes of the discounted cash flow technique, provoked by a problem in which the conventional tests gave no help. The economic principles which find expression in that technique have no doubt been long familiar to many others in industry who have also regarded the conventional tests as crude approximations, good enough for practical purposes. As the work went on, however, it became apparent to those engaged in it - accountants and economists - that in some situations of practical importance the use of the D C F technique would point to decisions different from, and more appropriate to our objective than, those indicated by the conventional tests; and that this technique must therefore be preferred. This conclusion was strengthened by the effects on our financial assessments of the tax changes which had been introduced since the study began with the object of encouraging investment. These effects could not be reflected adequately by the conventional tests but were brought clearly into focus by the use of the D C F technique.

Because of the unfamiliarity of the technique and the additional work it creates it seemed necessary to prepare carefully for any change in procedure if confusion was to be avoided. Messrs. Alfred and Evans therefore devised the short cut methods set out in this manual and conducted a series of one-day seminars to give practice in their use before the technique was formally adopted. This not only ensured a smooth transition; it also keeps the technique in its proper place and we hope to have avoided the experience of those firms which are said to have adopted the technique and later abandoned it because the mere arithmetic of it so dominated men's minds that other, more important aspects of their investment decisions were overlooked.

This manual is thus concerned with only part of investment appraisal and is not even a complete study of the D C F technique. It is no more than a guide to some short cuts in the use of that technique which one firm has found helpful. The recent N E D C publication on the subject recognises the need for such aids and all who have been active in this work have therefore been glad to co-operate in making the manual available for wider use.

January 1965

PREFACE TO THE THIRD EDITION

Our objective in this book has been to present in the simplest terms possible some of the short cut techniques that we in Courtaulds have found useful. But we have felt compelled, in a book for general publication, to introduce qualifications where necessary and, of course, to give many examples. We would not like this to blind the reader to the fact that, in many cases, a project can be approximated to one in which all expenditure occurs in a single year, followed by a constant cash flow, or a cash flow which declines by a given amount each year. These cases are covered by the graphs in Chapter 3 which can give a rough answer very quickly. Refinements necessary for a more accurate answer are given in the text, but this rough answer will often be adequate for the first 'thumbnail calculation' with which so many investment projects start.

All the short cut methods in the book assume that the company concerned will have sufficient liability to tax to enable it to take full benefit from capital allowances as soon as they are available. Where this is not the case, the D C F return must be calculated in full; Forms 1, 2, and 3 can be used, but not the Tax Tables associated with them.

Throughout the book, the examples and calculations are based on assumed tax conditions of a $42\frac{1}{2}\%$ Corporation Tax, and the system of investment grants and allowances introduced in October 1970. Rough adjustments for other tax conditions are also given.

In this third edition we are pleased to acknowledge the help of Mr. J. Connor who has been responsible for modifying the text and examples to take account of changes in the system of capital allowances. We also acknowledge the help of Mr. R. Cooper for assistance with the calculations.

A. M. A.
J. B. E.

February 1971

CONTENTS

* The Interest Tables are reproduced by kind permission of the Australian Society of Accountants.

Chapter 1 : The Principles and Advantages
of Discounted Cash Flow

I INTRODUCTION

Chapters 2 to 4 of this book discuss methods, as developed in Courtaulds Ltd., for the practical application of the discounted cash flow procedure. We think it is true to say that today there is no informed opinion which doubts the validity of the discounted cash flow (D C F) approach - witness the Report published by N E D C in 1965[a] - although there is certainly some argument on detail, and there may be more doubt about whether the extra effort involved is justified by the results. Chapters 2 to 4 will show that this extra effort need not be very much. In this chapter, we are concerned to illustrate that the results obtained are so significant both to an individual company and to the economic growth of the country, that, even if a lot of effort were required, it would certainly be justified. This is because the D C F approach leads to a marked change in the emphasis of investment policy, as compared with most traditional methods, in favour of investment in cost and labour-saving plant - and it is this which is the motive force of an expanding economy. This method is, therefore, put forward not just because it is theoretically superior, but because it has important practical consequences.

The graphs and examples in this book are based on the current rate of corporation tax of $42\frac{1}{2}\%$ and the rate of investment grants and allowances announced in October, 1970. Typically, these are:

	First Year Allowance (for plant)	or	Initial Allowance (for buildings)
PLANT : for manufacturing, etc.			
- ordinary location	60		-
- development area	100		-
INDUSTRIAL BUILDINGS:			
- ordinary location			15
- development area			40

An investment grant of 35% or 45% is available on buildings in a development area. Fuller details are given in the reference material in Chapter 5, section (c) - page 69.

Graphs are given for use with all these conditions. In addition, in chapters 3 and 4 we indicate the approximate effect of a 5% change in the rate of corporation tax. As the effect

---

a) See bibliography, reference 4.

of any grants is dealt with outside the graphs, and any change automatically catered for,
is anticipated that the short cut methods now presented will have validity for some consid
erable time.

II SOME TRADITIONAL METHODS OF ASSESSING INVESTMENT

4. Most firms still assess the worthwhileness of investment projects by considering such
things as:

(i) return on capital - defined usually as expected profit after allowing for depreciation,
but before tax, as a percentage of the investment involved. In some cases, the initia
investment is taken; in other cases, the average investment over the life of the proje
Where investment grants are available, there is the further ambiguity that the investment involved may be before or after deducting investment grant. In some cases
the profit is 'peak' profit; in other cases, average profit over the expected life.

(ii) payback period - number of years to recover the cost of the project, ignoring deprec
ation; sometimes calculated before tax and sometimes after tax.

5. These measures, even if taken together, are subject to a number of criticisms.
Return on capital: this suffers from:

(i) the difficulty of putting one figure to 'expected profit' in cases where the profit may
not be constant over the years.

(ii) the possibly misleading nature of depreciation, if it happens to differ (as in accounts
it usually does) from depreciation for tax purposes.

(iii) the difficulty of defining capital in any meaningful sense without taking account of the
very substantial recovery of capital expenditure from the Government as a result of
grants, initial and depreciation allowances. On manufacturing plant the total investm
is allowed against tax, and the capital recovered is $42\frac{1}{2}\%$. In a non-development
area 25% is recovered in the first year, and 35% within 4 years. In a development
area the whole $42\frac{1}{2}\%$ is received within the first year.

(iv) no specific account is taken of the earning life of the investment, i.e. the same answ
is sometimes returned whether profits are expected to be earned for a period of 5
years, 15 years or 25 years.

(v) no allowance is made for the fact that £1 tomorrow is worth less than £1 today.

Payback period: if calculated after tax and before depreciation, and taking account of ta
ation recoveries or savings, points (i), (ii) and (iii) above are met. But criticisms (iv) a
(v) remain.

The question of the earning life is sometimes met by adding to the considerations the 'number of years over which profitability is expected to be maintained'. Apart from the difficulty of defining this when profitability is not constant (except by giving a detailed schedule), it means that the assessment of a project would have to be considered by reference to at least three factors:

return on capital; payback period; period of full profitability;

with there being no precise method for balancing one against the other.

What is needed, therefore, is a method which can reduce to a single figure the above considerations for a particular project; with that figure being logically consistent with similar figures derived for other projects.

This is what the D C F approach does.

III OBJECTIVE IN ASSESSING CAPITAL PROJECTS

Before going on to describe the D C F method, it is worthwhile defining what a company seeks in its investment policy. The answer, we suggest, is the same as that looked for by any investor - the maximum net cash flow, i.e. after deducting taxation. And this cash flow must be sufficient to repay the initial outlay and to pay an adequate rate of interest on the balance outstanding at any time. The worthwhileness of the investment will, therefore, be expressed by the magnitude of the average effective rate of interest on the outstanding balances over the life of the investment. This is what is measured by the D C F method.

IV DISCOUNTED CASH FLOW

(a) The measurement of D C F

Having asserted that the D C F method overcomes the disadvantages of the traditional methods, and measures the average effective rate of interest on the outstanding balances over the life of the investment, it remains to illustrate how it does this, and what is the arithmetical procedure involved.

When an investment is made, it typically results in an estimated cash flow in the future. This cash flow will be compounded of:

profits, after tax; depreciation provisions; investment grants where applicable;

that otherwise would not accrue.

It is important to note the phrase 'that otherwise would not accrue'. If a company has sufficient taxable profits from other activities, the annual depreciation allowances applicable to a new investment can be offset against tax immediately, so the gain to a company is large. This is the typical situation, and is that assumed in the short-cut methods developed in Chapters 3 and 4. Where this is not the case, the benefit from capital allowances must await the build-up of profits from the new investment, and so is delayed, and hence is of less value. The receipt of the grants is independent of tax considerations, as they do not depend on an offsetting tax liability. It is completely justified from an individual company's viewpoint to take credit, in assessing a new investment, for the savings in tax payable on profits from existing assets. In all cases, the worthwhileness of any course of action must be measured by looking at the <u>cash flow position if the project takes place, compared with what otherwise would have happened.</u> And 'otherwise' the reduction in tax payments would not have occurred.

12. The incidence of these three items will vary significantly over the years, with tax savings in particular being concentrated in the early years. We are, therefore, faced with an irregular schedule of future cash benefits, which we need to relate to the original capital investment. We know, of course, that £1 in the future is worth less than £1 now and, if the project is one earning a true profit of, say, 10%, then, as far as this project concerned, £1 in a year's time is worth $1/1.10 = £0.91$ now. Similarly, £1 in two years time is worth only $1/(1.10)^2 = £0.83$ now, and so on.

Put another way, if the project results in a cash flow of £1 in 2 years' time, we could regard that as composed of a repayment of capital of £0.83 and interest at 10% p.a. compound for 2 years totalling £0.17. If this is done for the cash receipts for each year of the project and then totalled, we could then say that the project as a whole has yielded a repayment of capital of £X, and total interest payments corresponding to compound interest at 10%. By trial and error, we can clearly find the appropriate rate of interest which will leave the capital repayment at a total equal to the original investment. This rate of interest is the solution rate of interest for the project.

13. An example will illustrate:

Investment at end of year 0 : £31.7

Life of project : 4 years

Expected cash flow : £10 a year for 4 years

Solution rate of interest : 10%

Year	Cash Flow	Composed of		
		Compound interest at 10% p.a.		on a capital sum being repaid of:
		for no. of years	totalling	
	£		£	£
1	10	1	0.9	9.1
2	10	2	1.7	8.3
3	10	3	2.5	7.5
4	10	4	3.2	6.8
	40		8.3	31.7

The capital investment of £31.7 has been completely repaid; and total interest of £8.3 has been earned. This is shown in the above example to be equal to interest at 10% on the sums repaid. It is also equal to 10% on the outstanding balances at any time, as is illustrated below.

Year	Capital outstanding at beginning of year	10% interest on capital outstanding	Cash Flow	Capital Repayment
	£	£	£	£
1	31.7	3.2	10	6.8
2	24.9	2.5	10	7.5
3	17.4	1.7	10	8.3
4	9.1	0.9	10	9.1
		8.3	40	31.7

In paragraph 13, the deduction of an interest element from the cash flow is called 'discounting' it (in this case at 10% p.a.). Hence the name of the method - discounted cash flow.

The example is shown with a regular pattern of cash flow; but an irregular pattern presents no difficulties. To summarise, therefore, the D C F approach provides a ready means of:
(i)   taking account of the irregular pattern of tax savings;
(ii) recognising the importance of the time pattern of profits (and capital expenditure). Thus £10 received in year 4 would be worth only £6.8 in year 0 at a 10% discount rate;
(iii) forcing attention to be paid to 'cash' rather than 'profit after depreciation and before tax'. This is not attainable only by D C F methods, but any other method raises difficulties in taking account of tax payments.

(b)   The practical significance of D C F

D C F calculations, although simple in principle, take longer to calculate in practice. It is clear, therefore, that there is no point in changing to this method just because it is theoretically desirable, unless it really points to policy conclusions different from - or more clearly expressed than - those deduced from the traditional approach. And this it does.

18.   Later, in paras 31 - 32, we suggest that an average rate of return applicable to equity
      capital in private industry under the proposed corporation tax and capital gains system
      may be about 10% (after corporation tax, and in real terms, i.e. after allowing for the
      effect of price inflation). If, for the sake of illustration, we accept this figure, and
      assuming sufficient taxable profits available from other activities to give full benefit of
      capital allowances, it can be shown by an arithmetical example (see Appendix A) that this
      is the D C F return which is earned on a typical investment in a new activity with the
      following characteristics:
      (i)   investment 60% plant, 25% buildings, 15% working capital (or land).
      (ii) traditional profit (after depreciation, before tax) building up gradually to 15% return
            on the original investment by Year 4, maintaining this level for 4 years, and declining
            thereafter.

19.   If all investments were to have the relationship of D C F return to traditional return of
      10 : 15, there would clearly be no sense in changing to D C F calculations. However, the
      D C F return will be proportionately higher than the 10 : 15 ratio in cases where
      (i)   the plant content is more than 60% of total investment assumed in the attached
            example (because of the value of annual allowances given on investment in
            plant), and
      (ii) the earnings are high in the early years - instead of building up slowly to a peak in the
            fifth year.

20.   To illustrate (ii): for a project where all the expenditure is on plant and where the full ben
      accrues immediately the investment is complete, a 10% D C F return is equivalent to a
      traditional 'profit' (i.e. after depreciation, but before tax) of only 7% on the original cost
      (see Appendix B).

21.   In the case of the acquisition of a business, there are offsetting factors. The fact that
      profits start immediately is beneficial, but the absences of any allowances is adverse. If we
      assume that the ploughback of depreciation enables profits to be held at the current level
      indefinitely, the 10% D C F corresponds to pre-tax profits as a percentage of purchase
      price of 17%, i.e. 10% grossed up at the tax rate of $42\frac{1}{2}\%$ (see Appendix C).

22.   In other words, whereas, with traditional thinking, we may be looking for the same tradi-
      tional return on all three types of investment, we would now say that the following, under
      our current tax conditions, give really equal returns:

	Traditional return corresponding to 10% D C F
Project with slow build-up of profits to peak level, 10-year life (60% plant, 25% building, 15% working capital)	15%
Project - all plant, and profits constant from first year, 10-year life	7%
Company acquisition with depreciation ploughed back to maintain profits	17%

It should be emphasized that the above are illustrations only as they are dependent on the precise assumptions and lives detailed in the appendices.

The actual figures also depend on the 'traditional' measure taken. Here we have used the typical (or peak) profit as a percentage of original investment. But, under any traditional measure, the disparity shown above would be apparent, with, in each case, the real attractiveness of investment in plant being understated.

(c)   The value of D C F in special circumstances

Another advantage of the D C F technique is that it enables account to be taken of unusual factors. Thus, for development areas, the real effect of the free depreciation provision available on investment in·plant, and the grants on buildings, can be calculated. For example, Appendix B shows that an investment in plant in an ordinary location will have a 10% D C F return with a constant gross cash flow of 17% of the original outlay (i. e. 7% traditional return plus 10% depreciation). A similar investment in a development area, receiving the free depreciation provision, will have a 10% D C F return with only a 16% constant gross cash flow. In the case of buildings in a development area, a grant of 35% and an initial allowance of 40% means that the effective cost of a building (with a purchase price of £100 and 20-year life) is only £49, instead of the £79 it would cost in an ordinary location. (N. B. Effective cost is measured net of grant, the value of annual allowances, and residual value; a 10% discount factor is used. See Chapter 4 graphs C and D.)   The D C F technique also enables a precise measure to be given to the effect of general tax changes, such as the introduction of grants or other changes in allowances. *

g. see refs. (9) and (10).

26. Another useful illustration of the use of D C F principles is where it is required to calcula[te] the maximum price one company can afford to pay for the acquisition of another. This pri[ce] will be that which allows the buyer to earn a return just equal to his cost of capital. Appen[dix] C shows the method in the simple case where it is assumed that the 'profit' is constant for[an] unlimited number of years. In most cases, however, an acquisition is considered becaus[e it] may allow the exploitation of a special position, e.g. a merging of sales forces, or of re-search, or economies in production. The anticipated cash benefit is anything but constant. [In] such a case, it is necessary to estimate just what net cash savings or extra profits (after allowing for tax) might accrue year by year. This cash flow is then discounted at the com[-]pany's cost of capital to give a 'present value' of the future cash flow. In the example in p[age] 13, the cash flow of £10 p.a. in years 1 to 4 has a total present value after discounting at 10% of £31.7. This means, as para 14 shows, that £31.7 invested in such a project woul[d] earn a return of 10% p.a. over and above that needed to repay the initial investment. It fol[lows] that, if a company were seeking a 10% return, and calculated the benefit of an acquisition [or] any other investment) to be £10 p.a. for 4 years, it could afford to pay up to £31.7. And £31.7 was obtained by calculating the present value at 10% discount of the future cash flow[.] This alternative to calculating the solution rate of interest is useful in any situation where the object is to determine the maximum cost one can afford for a given benefit. It is also useful in some other cases - (para 29 (iii)).

(d) The limitations of D C F ?

27. The limitations sometimes voiced are both practical and theoretical. The practical objec-tion that it may be cumbersome and time-consuming is dealt with in Chapters 2 to 4 of this book. We believe that the system now employed in Courtaulds, using the standard forms and graphs given later, enable us to get approximate answers in simple cases in a matter of minutes, and answers to more complicated projects in half an hour. More time may be required to elucidate the assumptions (of future price levels, costs, length of life, etc.) necessary to evaluate the cash inflow; but an appreciation of these basic assumptions shoul[d] be a pre-requisite of any investment decision. Indeed, we have found that the discipline en[-]forced by the application of D C F has been one of its useful by-products.

There is, however, an associated objection. To enable a D C F calculation to be done, the project has to be defined in its entirety - cash flow each year (usually involving detailed volume, price and cost assumptions), length of life, tax allowances, scrap values, etc. This sometimes suggests an air of accuracy - which is, of course, completely spurious. No techniques, however sound, can foretell the future. All that D C F does is to enable the correct conclusions to be drawn from the assumptions. But nevertheless, we should face the fact that some people associate the volume of arithmetic with the accuracy of the result. To overcome this, we suggest strongly that any major investment decision should be examined in D C F terms on three sets of assumptions - 'most likely', 'better' and 'worse'. This is the basis on which the form in Chapter 5(a) has been drawn up. The range of returns shown indicates the sensitivity of the return to changes in the assumptions, and this can give an idea of the project's degree of risk.

The theoretical objections are said to be that:

(i) the calculation of the solution rate of interest implies that funds realised throughout the life of the project should be reinvested at the solution rate. This view is widely held, but consideration of the examples in paras 12 and 13, where the solution rate of 10% is determined by discounting the cash flow each year at 10% p. a., shows that there is no implication of re-investing at 10% interest the £10 received each year.

(ii) in certain cases, it is possible to get more than one solution rate, which are then both meaningless. This is true in the rare cases where a large outflow of funds (investment) follows a large inflow of funds. But even in these cases, there is a simple expedient for overcoming this difficulty (see Bibliography reference (1)).

(iii) in choosing between mutually exclusive projects, i.e. where only one of two or more are possible, it may be wrong to choose the project with the highest solution rate. This is true because, for example, it may be better to choose to invest:

(a) £1,000 at 18% return rather than £100 at 20% return for the same period; or

(b) £1,000 at 18% return for 10 years, rather than £1,000 at 20% return for 2 years.

These special cases can be treated by alternative methods, such as evaluating the profitability of the difference between the two alternatives, or finding the 'present value' of each project discounted at the minimum desired rate of return. The project with the greater excess of present value over the cost of the investment is the one which is more attractive.

30.   It is clear, therefore, that we believe there are no serious limitations to the comprehensive use of D C F principles. But, in Courtaulds, we nevertheless still use it to supple-
ment traditional methods, such as payback and peak-return on initial capital, rather than
replace them entirely (see Form in Chapter 5(a) - item 7).

V   THE ACCEPTABLE RATE OF RETURN

31.   We do not intend, in this, a book on the practical application of D C F, to enter into a full
theoretical discussion of this factor. Elsewhere* it was shown that, under the old system
of taxation (of income tax and profits tax), 7% D C F (after tax and in real terms) was a
typical cost of equity capital to a public company, and hence the minimum acceptable rate
of return. It was also the return enjoyed by a shareholder paying the standard rate of
income tax. This accords roughly with the history of the last 40 years** and corresponds
with a reasonable expectation looking forward. However, the introduction of corporation
and capital gains taxes produces a distinction between the return earned by a company and
that earned by its shareholders, as the personal tax (of 7s. 9d. per £) is paid by the shar-
holder on the gross dividend distributed by the company. Alternatively, if earnings are
ploughed back, the accretion in value of the share is subject to a capital gains tax at the
time of realisation. If shareholders are to continue to earn 7% D C F, a company will now
have to earn significantly more.*** On retained earnings, a company would have to earn
about $8\frac{1}{2}\%$; and on money raised by new issues a company may have to earn 11-12%, depen-
ing on its distribution policy. Its overall requirement on equity capital will depend on the
extent to which a company is dependent on new issues, and may change from time to time.
A representative figure may be around 10%. This is the rate of return, in real terms,
that companies need to earn on their equity if they are to use capital with an average degr
of efficiency; and this is the figure used in the illustration in paragraph 22.

---

*   Bibliography ref. (8)
**   Bibliography ref. (6)
***   See Chapter 4 of ref. (5)

The discussion so far has not dealt specifically with the question of risk. Specific companies and industries operate in different environments with regard to risk. Where risk is significantly greater than for average industry, a company may need to aim at a higher rate of return on its investment programme taken as a whole.

The only important exception to the rate of return suggested above is where there is heavy dependence on borrowed funds at a fixed interest rate. Under the corporation tax system, preference capital with a coupon of, say, 8% costs the company the full 8% (after corporation tax). Bank loans or debenture capital with a nominal interest rate of 8% would cost a company only 4.6% net, because the interest is allowable against corporation tax at $42\frac{1}{2}\%$. In both cases, this is in money terms. If there is price inflation, the real cost of fixed interest capital will fall. For example, if the rate of inflation is 2% p.a., the real cost of loan capital may be 2.6% compared with the 10% for equity capital suggested above.

It must be recognised that the above figures are in real terms, i.e., the effect of price changes has been eliminated. And it is our recommendation that all calculations be done in real terms. This means that the general level of prices is assumed unchanged, although, of course, the price of the product involved in the project may change relative to general prices. Wages, however, can be expected to rise in real terms, by 2-3% p.a., depending on the growth of the national economy; and this growth in real wages should be taken into account in calculating future profits where wages are a significant cost factor.

The following Chapters 2, 3 and 4 give actual examples of the application of D C F principles to a range of investment projects. For those who wish to practise our methods, it will be necessary for them to have blank copies of Forms 1, 2, and 3, and of the interpolation chart.

In the first instance, while understanding of the method is being gained, we recommend that the 'longhand' method in Chapter 2 be followed. For similar reasons, while recognizing the contribution that computers can make to easing calculations, we feel that their use should not become a routine until the D C F principles are fully understood.

CHAPTER 1 : PRINCIPLES

VI SOME TECHNICAL FACTORS

37. In order not to clutter the main text, we give separately below some more technical comment.

  (i) <u>Inflation</u> Para 34 discusses how to handle growth in real wages. Inflation as such (i.e. wage and price increases of the same amount) is nearly neutral in its effect on future profits, because there will usually be rises in both costs and prices. However, because grants and other capital allowances are related to historical cost, their benefit falls in a time of inflation, and the real return on a project is slightly depressed - but by not more than $\frac{1}{2}$% or so. In some cases where payments or receipts are fixed in money terms (such as leasing), inflation could, of course, have a greater effect.

  (ii) <u>Method of discounting</u> The tables given in Chapter 5(d) are based on end-year discounting, i.e. they assume that all cash inflow or outflow occurs on the last day of the year. This is a convenient, although arbitrary assumption. It introduces very little error provided both the inflow and outflow calculations are calculated on the same basis.

  (iii) <u>The distinction between an individual investment project and a capital programme</u> After determining the cost of capital, this becomes the minimum acceptable rate for investment There will, however, be some occasions where an individual project which is expected to earn more than this minimum should be rejected. This is where it forms part of a capital programme where the programme as a whole (including non-profit earners such as amenities, and effluent treatment) is expected to earn less than the cut-off point. Under these circumstances, <u>no</u> projects within that programme, however profitable individually, should be allowed to proceed. The long-term viability of the operation as a whole should be examined.

Year	(1) Plant	(2) Investment Buildings	(3) Working Capital	(4) Allowances for Tax 1st Year and initial Allowances	(5) Allowances for Tax Subsequent Years	(6) Tax saved 42.5% x (4)+(5)	(7)* Notional Depreciation	(8)* Profit	(9) Profit before Depreciation	(10) Tax on (9)	(11) NET CASH OUTFLOW (1)+(2)+(3)	(12) NET CASH INFLOW (6)+(9)−(10)	9% Discount Factors	9% Outflow	9% Inflow	11% Discount Factors	11% Outflow	11% Inflow
0	30	12·5	10	19·9							42·5		1·000	42·5		1·000	42·5	
1	30	12·5	5	19·9		8·5	7·0	(−7·0)(i)			52·5	8·5	·917	48·0	7·8	·901	47·3	7·7
2					3·5	10·0	7·0	7·0	14·0		5·0	24·0	·842	4·2	20·2	·812	4·1	19·5
3					6·2	2·6	7·0	12·0	19·0	6·0		15·6	·772		12·0	·731		11·4
4					5·0	2·1	7·0	15·0	22·0	8·1		16·0	·708		11·3	·659		10·5
5					4·0	1·7	7·0	15·0	22·0	9·3		14·4	·650		9·4	·593		8·5
6					3·3	1·4	7·0	15·0	22·0	9·3		14·1	·596		8·4	·535		7·6
7					2·7	1·1	7·0	15·0	22·0	9·3		13·8	·547		7·6	·482		6·7
8					2·2	0·9	7·0	12·0	19·0	9·3		10·6	·502		5·3	·434		4·6
9					1·9	0·8	7·0	7·0	14·0	8·1		6·7	·460		3·1	·391		2·6
10	(−3·0)(d)	(−15·5)(e)	(−15)(k)		1·7	0·7	7·0	1·0	8·0	6·0		36·2(j)	·422		15·3	·352		12·7
11					(−3·7)(f)	(−1·6)				3·4		(−5·0)	·388		(−1·9)	·317		(−1·6)
				39·8	26·8	28·2	70·0	92·0	162	68·8	100	154·9		94·7	98·5		93·9	90·2

Conclusion	at 9% disc.	at 11% disc.
A. Investment (Cash Outflow)	94·7	93·9
B. Receipts (Cash Inflow)	98·5	90·2
Ratio A/B	·96	1·04

The D C F solution rate is the rate at which the investment is exactly recovered, i.e. cash inflow equals cash outflow, i.e. A/B = 1·0. By interpolation the D C F RATE OF RETURN is about 10%

TRADITIONAL RETURN is 15% i.e. peak profit after depreciation as a percentage of the cost of the investment

Notes:

(a) Initial allowance for buildings of 15% and first year allowance on plant of 60%, each received one year after expenditure.

(b) Annual allowance for plant is 25% reducing balance. Annual allowance for buildings is 4% (straight line). The annual allowances begin in year 2, as the project is assumed to begin operating in year 1.

(c) The total tax saved as a result of capital allowances is treated as a cash receipt. It is important to note that this is only valid if the company undertaking the project has sufficient profits overall to absorb the capital allowances as soon as they arise – or if subvention payments can be made.

(d) Scrap value assumed equal to 5% of original cost.

(e) Residual value of buildings. This is assumed to equal the written-down value after straight line depreciation at 4% per annum.

(f) This is the difference between the tax written-down value of the plant (2.1) and building (12.7) and their respective residual values.

(g) Depreciation of plant is straight-line over 10 years, buildings over 25 years.

(h) Tax at 42½% lagged one year for payment.

(i) i.e. assumed cash break-even in year 1.

(j) Includes recoveries from scrap and of working capital (columns 1-3).

(k) Assuming working capital is fully recovered at end of the project.

* These columns are unnecessary if figures of profit before depreciation are available directly.

A Typical Project of **ALL PLANT** with **PROFITS CONSTANT** at 7%

Year	(1) Investment in Plant	(2) Annual Tax Allowances (a)	(3) Tax Saved 42½% x (2) (b)	(4)* Notional Depreciation (c)	(5)* Profit	(6) Profit before Depreciation	(7) Tax on (6) (d)	(8) NET CASH OUTFLOW (1)	(9) NET CASH INFLOW (3)+(6)−(7)	Cash Flow Discounted at 10% — Discount Factors	Outflow	Inflow
0	100							100		1·000	100	
1		60	25·5	10	7·0	17·0	7·2		42·5	·909		38·6
2		10	4·3	10	7·0	17·0	7·2		14·1	·826		11·7
3		7·5	3·2	10	7·0	17·0	7·2		13·0	·751		9·8
4		5·6	2·4	10	7·0	17·0	7·2		12·2	·663		8·3
5		4·2	1·8	10	7·0	17·0	7·2		11·6	·621		7·2
6		3·2	1·3	10	7·0	17·0	7·2		11·1	·564		6·3
7		2·4	1·0	10	7·0	17·0	7·2		10·8	·513		5·5
8		1·8	0·8	10	7·0	17·0	7·2		10·6	·467		5·0
9		1·3	0·6	10	7·0	17·0	7·2		10·4	·424		4·4
10		1·0	0·4	10	7·0	17·0	7·2		15·2(e)	·386		5·9
11	(−5)(c)	(−2·0)(g)	(−0·9)		7·0	17·0	7·2		(−8·1)	·350		(−2·8)
		95·0(f)	40·4	100	70·0	170·0	72·0		143·4		100	99·9

TRADITIONAL RETURN is 7 on investment of 100 = 7%

Conclusion

As the discounted values of inflow and outflow are nearly equal, the D C F RATE OF RETURN is about 10%

Notes:

(a) Annual allowance is 60% in year 1 and 25% reducing balance thereafter.

(b) The total tax saved as a result of capital allowances is treated as a cash receipt. It is important to note that this is only valid if the company undertaking the project has sufficient profits overall to absorb the capital allowances as soon as they arise - or if subvention payments can be made.

(c) Scrap value of plant, assumed to be 5% of cost.

(d) 42½% of column (6) lagged one year.

(e) Includes recovery of scrap value.

(f) Equals cost less scrap value.

(g) This is the difference between the written-down value (3.0) and the scrap value.

* These columns are unnecessary if figures of profit before depreciation are available directly.

PURCHASE OF EXISTING COMPANY

The following assumptions are made:

(a) depreciation provisions are ploughed back and are just sufficient to maintain profits at their current level indefinitely.

(b) the tax charge is $42\frac{1}{2}\%$.

Because of assumption (a), the cash flow attributable to the investment is profit after depreciation, and the net cash flow is this amount less tax. Since a perpetual annuity of x% by definition gives a D C F return of x% on the price paid for the annuity, it follows that, under these conditions, a company must have earnings of 10% (after depreciation and tax) on the purchase price to give a 10% D C F return.

These net earnings of 10% correspond to gross profits - after depreciation and before corporation tax - of 17% (i.e. 10% grossed up at $42\frac{1}{2}\%$ tax rate). *

assuming book depreciation is in line with depreciation for tax purposes.

Chapter 2 : DCF Method in full

I INTRODUCTION

This chapter describes the method for calculating the D C F return on a project by deriving a figure for each individual year's cash flow, each figure representing the net effect of the project on the company's cash position in that year. This schedule of cash flow figures is then discounted at various rates, and the D C F return found by interpolation, of which an illustration is given in Appendix A of Chapter 1.

When we talk of the D C F return on a project, we normally refer to the total return irrespective of the method of financing. The cash flows are therefore normally before deducting interest payments etc. The effect of fixed interest borrowing is reflected in the determination of the cost of capital as indicated in Chapter 1.

II METHOD OUTLINED

The basic ingredients generally necessary to derive the D C F return on a project are:

investment;   profit before depreciation; and

recoveries at the end of the project (e.g., scrap value of plant and working capital) Given an estimate of these, the figures need to be 'processed' to put them on an after-tax basis, and any investment grants which are receivable deducted from expenditure. Much of the laboriousness of D C F calculations is concerned with these processes, but Tax Tables giving the effect of capital allowances shorten the task considerably. These are given at the end of this chapter for typical situations of plant and buildings; namely:

for plant: subject to 60% allowance in the first year and 25% annual allowance
            thereafter: Table 1

for buildings: subject to either 15% or 40% initial allowance, and 4% annual
            allowance: Table II

The tables show the year-by-year net tax saving which the net investment (after deducting any grant) yields to a company with <u>enough profits to absorb all its allowances</u>. In the case of buildings different savings are given according to the year in which the investment becomes operational (since this determines when the first annual allowance is available). The table on plant also gives the amount of tax still unrecovered after any number of years, the whole of this (less some deduction if there is any scrap value) being claimable as soon as the project ends. A note is appended to Table II to allow similar information to be calculated for buildings. These tables are such that they can be used with any level of grant, and so are applicable to both Development Areas and ordinary locations. Explanatory notes are appended to each table indicating how they are to be used.

4.   It is desirable to build up the final schedule of annual net cash flows in a systematic way to prevent any errors of 'method' being introduced. For this purpose we use standard forms (see Forms 1 and 2 at the end of the chapter) which are largely self-explanatory. Form 1 gives the expenditure and derives the net tax saved. Recoveries (i.e. scrap and residual values of plant and buildings, and recovery of working capital) are also entered on this form. An allowance should be made for any grants by treating them as a deduction from expenditure. Grants should be deducted at the time of their receipt, which is normally one year after the relevant expenditure. Form 2 draws together the cash outflow and the cash inflow. The cash outflow is taken from column 7 of Form 1. The cash inflow is built up from gross profits before depreciation (column 3) less the tax on these (column 4) plus the net tax saved and the recoveries, brought from Form 1. These flows are then discounted at various trial rates to enable the D C F returns to be calculated.

III   PROCEDURE IN DETAIL

5.   The procedure can best be illustrated by following the steps involved in calculating the return on a hypothetical project. We have taken here that given on the form headed 'Application for sanction of an investment project' to be found in Chapter 5. The project is <u>outside</u> a Development Area.

6.   <u>Expenditure</u>   The expenditure data is given in item 13 of the Application Form. This is entered in Form 1. The first year's expenditure is, of course, entered opposite year 0, which in this project is 1970. The total cash outflow by years is taken from column 7 to the top of Form 2. (N.B. If the example had been within a development area, the buildings would receive a grant. This would be allowed for by deducting the grant from the expenditure, to derive net expenditure which is transferred to Form 2. The grant should be treated as being received one year after the relevant expenditure.)

7.   <u>Tax Savings</u>   We assume that the company concerned can absorb the capital allowances arising from this project. The savings can then be calculated from the Tax Tables, by applying the percentages given in the tables to the individual items of expenditure shown columns 1 - 4 (of Form 1). We assume here that all plant and buildings first come into operation in 1971 (i.e. 'year after purchase' for all 1970 expenditure, and 'year of purch

for 1971 expenditure). Taking the plant purchased in 1970 which is eligible for a 60% first year allowance with a 25% annual allowance thereafter, the expenditure is £280.

From Table I the tax savings are then -

Year 1 25.5% x 280 = 72
Year 2 4.3% x 280 = 12
Year 3 3.2% x 280 = 9 etc.

These figures are entered in column 8. Column 9 derives in a similar way, using Table 1, the savings on the £200 spent in year 1 (operating in 'year of purchase'). These are:

Year 2 25.5% x 200 = 51
Year 3 4.3% x 200 = 9 etc.

Column 11 gives the tax savings on the £170 expenditure on buildings. These are based on Table II, with 15%* initial allowance and using the column 'year after purchase'. Thus,

Year 1 6.4 x 170 = 11
Year 2 1.7 x 170 = 3 etc.

The project ends in year 10, so that in the following year all the remaining allowances become available. On the £280 these amount to 1.2% (see the third column of Tax Table I, opposite year 10) or £3.4. The realised £14 for scrap value is, however, subject to tax, giving a tax charge of £6 (at $42\frac{1}{2}$% tax rate). Thus the net saving in year 11 is £3.4 - £6 = (-)£2.6. Note that on the £200 spent on plant in year 1, the balance of allowances at the end of year 10 of the project is 1.6%. That figure has been read off opposite year 9 of the tax table, because that is how long this particular piece of plant has been in existence. In short, the Tax Tables refer to 'plant' years, which must not be confused with 'project' years (on Form 1).

Residual Values Estimates have to be made of the values to be put on plant, buildings and working capital at the end of the project's life. On plant a 5% scrap value is typical. Working capital is assumed to be recovered in full at the end of the project's life.** On buildings, unless there are special factors, we take as a reasonable allowance for the value at the

---

This example is based on a 15% initial allowance for buildings in ordinary locations. This level of allowance will be given on expenditure incurred after April 5th 1972. Building expenditure prior to that date will receive a 30% initial allowance. Whilst the tables in this book are not based on a 30% initial allowance, they can easily be adjusted - see the notes following Table II.

Sometimes part could be recovered earlier, if for example the project were expected to move to a level of lower capacity working half way through its life.

end of the life of the project the expenditure (net of any grant) less depreciation at 4% per year. If there are special factors such as the building being designed solely for the project in mind, it may have no residual value; but there will be the compensatory balance of tax allowances to be claimed.

10. Net Cash Flows We are now in a position to total the cash outflows and cash inflows on Form 2. The cash outflow figures (£470, £250, etc.) are transferred from column 7 of Form 1. The residual values in the final year (in this case year 10) of columns 1 - 6 of Form 1 are totalled, and the amount (£251) transferred to column 6 of Form 2. The capital allowances are transferred from column 15 of Form 1 to column 5 of Form 2. Next, columns 1 - 3 are completed with the data on profits and depreciation which is given, or implicit, in the Application Form. Since column 3 is simply the addition of columns 1 and 2, there is clearly no need to fill in the first two columns if the original data already includes the figures of profit before depreciation. But if the profit figures have been calculated after depreciation, it becomes necessary to add back depreciation to each year's profit figure.

11. In this case the basic estimates were of profit before depreciation. These are recorded in column 3 of Form 2. Year 1 reflects a cash loss on start-up of £35. Depreciation is shown in column 2 and hence in column 1 profit after depreciation. The depreciation charge is based on a 10 year life for plant (giving £48) and a 25 year life for buildings (giving £6.8), a total depreciation charge of approximately £55. Tax on the profit before depreciation is then calculated and entered in the following year of column 4, since on average there is a one year time lag between profits being earned and tax being paid on them. Note that in year 2 there is a 'negative' tax payment of £15 on the cash loss of £35 in year 1. Finally, column 7 is completed, combining all the earlier calculations into single net cash flow figures for each year of the project. The 'negative' tax payment of £15 in year 2 is, of course, included as a positive item, as though it were an ordinary tax saving.

12. Discounting Only at this stage does discounting begin. Each year's cash outflow and net cash inflow is discounted by multiplying it by the discount factors printed on Form 2. Only four of the five discount rates shown need be used. For most projects (as this one) 5 to 20% are relevant; but for highly profitable projects it would be necessary to use the top

four rates. When the cash figures of outflow and inflow have thus been converted into their discounted value at four rates, the 'resultant' columns are totalled, e.g. at 5% the totals are £775 and £996. If, at any rate of discount, the two totals are equal, then that is the D C F return. In this case the return clearly falls between 10%, when the capital has been over-recovered by £31, and 15% where it has been under-recovered by £103. To find the exact answer, we need to calculate the ratios of (discounted) outflow and inflow, the object being to derive the rate of discount at which the ratio is unity, i.e. cash outflow and cash inflow are equal. For this project, we calculate the ratios to be 0.78, 0.96, 1.16 and 1.37. These ratios are then plotted on the Interpolation Chart (following Form 2) a smooth curve being drawn through the four points. From the point where the curve crosses the thick vertical line over the value of 1.0 on the horizontal axis, the D C F return can be read off on the vertical axis. In this case it is 11%.

IV VARYING THE ASSUMPTIONS

Variations on the main underlying assumption often do not necessitate complete recalculations of the D C F return, but simply adjustments to Form 2. For example, the 'worse' assumption given for this project in the Application Form was that prices would be 5% lower from 1975 onwards, or for project years 5 to 10. The only effect this variation has on the basic data is to alter columns 1 to 4 on Form 2; but rather than work Form 2 completely, a simple short-cut is available. The 5% price fall is on a turnover of £1030 (Application Form - item 15) and so is equivalent to £52 of profit before tax. This reduction is for years 5 to 10. Considering the effect of 10% discount, and ignoring tax, our original total inflow of £788 is reduced by -

$$
\begin{array}{ll}
\text{Year 5} & £52 \times 0.621 \\
\text{Year 6} & £52 \times 0.564 \\
\cdots\cdots\cdots\cdots\cdots \\
\text{Year 10} & £52 \times 0.386 \\
\hline
\text{Total} & £52 \times 2.975^* = £155
\end{array}
$$

To allow for the year's time lag in paying tax we first discount the tax rate of $42\frac{1}{2}\%$ for one year, i.e. $42\frac{1}{2}\% \times .909 = 38.6\%$. The tax 'saved' on the reduction in profits is thus 38.6% of

the sum of a series of consecutive discount factors can be determined from the Interest Tables in Chapter 5 (d). In this case, from Interest Table B, under 10% we see
Sum of discount factors for years 1 to 10   =   6.145
Sum of discount factors for years 1 to 4   =   3.170
Hence discount factors for years 5 to 10   =   2.975

£155, or £60. The net effect of the price fall is thus to reduce the cash inflow at 10% discount by £155 - £60 = £95, i.e. to a new figure of £693. When this process has been repeated at the four rates of discount, new ratios A/B are calculated and a new D C F return found. In this case it is 7.8%.

V   ILLUSTRATIVE CALCULATION OF D C F AND REFERENCE TABLES

	(1)	(2)	(3)	(4)	(5)	(6)	
PROJECT YEAR	NET EXPENDITURE						
	PLANT	BUILDINGS			ALLIED REVENUE EXPEND-ITURE	WORKING CAPITAL	TOT E) IT F 1
		Gross Expend-iture	Grants Receiv-able	Net Expend-iture			
0	280	170		170	20		
1	200					50	
2						50	
3						25	
4							
5							
6							
7							
8							
9							
10	(-24)(a)			(-102)(b)		(-125)	
11							
12							
13							
14							
15							
16							
17							
18							
19							
20							
21							
22							
23							
24							
25							
26							

(a) Scrap value, assumed at 5% of cost.

(b) Residual value, taken as original cost less straight line depreciation over 25 years, i.e. 100% - 10 x 4% = 60% of original cost.

* Recoveries (i.e. scrap and residual values of plant and buildings and recoveries of

(a) To be completed from Tax Table 1 in the case of plant eligible for 60% first-year a expenditure figure multiplied by the tax rate and lagged one year.

(b) To be completed from Tax Table II choosing 11 (a) for buildings eligible for 15% in

(c) $42\frac{1}{2}\%$ of column 5 lagged one year.

(9)	(10)	(11)	(12)	(13)	(14)	(15)
NET TAX SAVED RESULTING FROM EXPENDITURE						
ANT PURCHASED (a)		BUILDINGS PURCHASED (b)			ALLIED REVENUE EXPEND-ITURE (c)	TOTALS TO FORM 2 - COL. 5
Year 1	Year 2	Year 0	Year 1	Year 2		
		11.0			8.5	91.5
51.0		3.0				66.0
9.0		3.0				21.0
6.0		3.0				16.0
5.0		3.0				13.0
4.0		3.0				11.0
3.0		3.0				9.0
2.0		3.0				7.0
2.0		3.0				7.0
1.0		3.0				5.0
$(-1.0)^{(d)}$		$(-8.0)^{(e)}$				(-12.0)

Calculation of Balancing Allowances.

	(footnote reference)	(c)	(d)	(e)
No. of years of life of plant or building		10	9	10
Balance of allowances from Tax Tables (%)		1.2	1.6	20.8
		£	£	£
Value of balance of allowances		3.4	3.2	35.4
less tax at 42½% on residual value		6.0	4.3	43.4
		(-2.6)	(-1.1)	(-8.0)

...ld be entered as appropriate in columns 1 to 6 in the final year of the project.

...or plant attracting 100% first-year allowance is simply the appropriate net

...1(b) for buildings eligible for 40% initial allowance.

= 25 =

CASH FLOW SCHEDULE

A: CASH OUTFLOW

YEAR	CASH OUTFLOW from Form I col. 7	
0	470	
1	250	
2	50	
3	25	
		TOTALS [A]

B: CASH INFLOW

YEAR	(1) Profit	(2) Depreciation	(3) PROFIT BEFORE DEPRECIA-TION	(4) TAX at 42½% on previous year of col. 3	(5) TAX SAVED on allowances (from Form 1 col. 15)	(6) Recovery of capital (from final year of cols. 1-7 Form-1)	(7) NET CASH INFLOW 3+5+6−4
0				−	−		
1	(−90)	55	(−35)		91		56
2	10	55	65	(−15)	66		146
3	115	55	170	28	21		163
4	175	55	230	72	16		174
5	175	55	230	98	13		145
6	175	55	230	98	11		143
7	145	55	200	98	9		111
8	95	55	150	85	7		72
9	65	55	120	64	7		63
10	5	55	60	51	5	251	265
11				26	(−12)		(−38)
12							
13							
14							
15							
16							
17							
18							
19							
20							
21							
22							
23							
24							
25							
26							

TOTALS [B]	
RATIOS A/B	

DISCOUNTED AT 5%		DISCOUNTED AT 10%		DISCOUNTED AT 15%		DISCOUNTED AT 20%		DISCOUNTED AT 40%	
Factor	Resultant	Factor	Resultant	Factor	Resultant	Factor	Resultant	Factor	Resultant
1.0	470	1.0	470	1.0	470	1.0	470	1.0	
.952	238	.909	227	.870	218	.833	208	.714	
.907	45	.826	41	.756	38	.694	35	.510	
.864	22	.751	19	.658	16	.579	14	.364	
	775		757		742		727		

DISCOUNTED AT 5%		DISCOUNTED AT 10%		DISCOUNTED AT 15%		DISCOUNTED AT 20%		DISCOUNTED AT 40%	
Factor	Resultant	Factor	Resultant	Factor	Resultant	Factor	Resultant	Factor	Resultant
1.0		1.0		1.0		1.0		1.0	
.952	53	.909	51	.870	49	.833	48	.714	
.907	132	.826	120	.756	110	.694	101	.510	
.864	140	.751	122	.658	107	.579	94	.364	
.823	143	.683	119	.572	100	.482	84	.260	
.784	113	.621	90	.497	72	.402	58	.186	
.746	107	.564	81	.432	62	.335	48	.133	
.711	79	.513	57	.376	42	.279	31	.095	
.677	49	.467	34	.327	24	.233	17	.068	
.645	41	.424	27	.284	18	.194	12	.048	
.614	163	.386	102	.247	66	.162	43	.035	
.585	−22	.350	(−13)	.215	(−8)	.135	(−5)	.025	
.557		.319		.187		.112		.018	
.530		.290		.163		.093		.013	
.505		.263		.141		.078		.009	
.481		.239		.123		.065		.006	
.458		.218		.107		.054		.005	
.436		.198		.093		.045		.003	
.416		.180		.081		.038		.002	
.396		.164		.070		.031		.002	
.377		.149		.061		.026		.001	
.359		.135		.053		.022		.001	
.342		.123		.046		.018		.001	
.326		.112		.040		.015			
.310		.102		.035		.013			
.295		.092		.030		.010			
.280		.082		.025		.008			
	998		790		642		531		
	0·78		0·96		1·16		1·37		

D.C.F. SOLUTION RATE is where ratio
A/B = 1.0: by interpolation from graph =   **11·0 %**

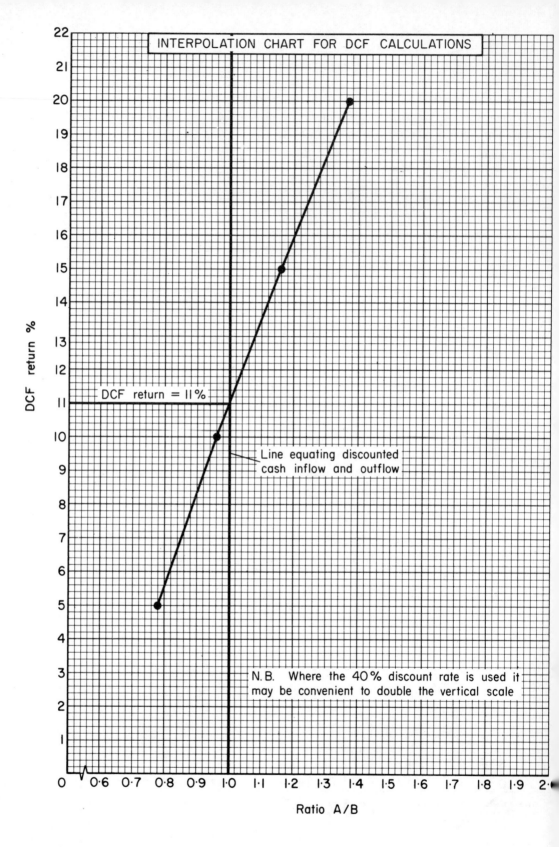

INTERPOLATION CHART FOR DCF CALCULATIONS

DCF return = 11%

Line equating discounted cash inflow and outflow

N.B. Where the 40% discount rate is used it may be convenient to double the vertical scale

DCF return %

Ratio A/B

Tax Table I

ALLOWANCES ON EXPENDITURE ON PLANT

Tax saved as a % of cost

60% 1st year allowance,
25% annual allowance thereafter,
tax rate $42\frac{1}{2}\%$

Number of years after purchase	Capital Allowances	Balance of Allowances remaining
1	25·5	17
2	4·3	12·7
3	3·2	9·5
4	2·4	7·1
5	1·8	5·3
6	1·3	4·0
7	1·0	3·0
8	0·8	2·2
9	0·6	1·6
10	0·4	1·2
11	0·3	0·9
12	0·2	0·7
13	0·2	0·5
14	0·1	0·4
15	0·1	0·3
16	0·3	
	42·5	

CHAPTER 2 : METHOD IN FULL

Notes to Table I (PLANT)

1. This schedule of tax savings is based on the current Corporation Tax rate of $42\frac{1}{2}\%$. Adjustments for different tax rates are given in note 6. If, at any time, grants are made available, this schedule can still be used but the savings are based on NET expenditure.

2. It can only be used as an aid to calculating the D C F return on a project provided the company can take advantage of the tax allowances as soon as they arise. Thus it must either have sufficient profits of its own to absorb the allowances, or be in a position to receive subvention payments from another company within the Group.

3. The first-year allowance of 60% is given for the financial year in which the expenditure is incurred - that is, it is given irrespective of the date at which the plant first comes into service. The table gives two sets of information; the second column shows the tax savings during the life of the project, and column 3 lists the balance of allowances still remaining at the end of a given year.

4. Column 2 of the table should be used to calculate the year-by-year allowances arising during the life of the project. The years in the left-hand column of the table refer to the number of years after the money is spent on the plant under consideration, and are not necessarily the same as the 'project years' in the left-hand columns of Forms 1 and 2 (which refer to the number of years after any money is spent on the project). Thus if money is spent in project year 2 the first tax saving can be found by looking at year 1 of the Table (under the appropriate column) but this is entered in year 3 of the project.

5. When a project is terminated (which in many cases will be before the 16 years covered in the Table), we use column 3 of the table to obtain the 'balance of allowances remaining' for the year in which the project ends. This is the net tax that could be claimed, subject to any realisation from scrap. We therefore have to deduct from it $42\frac{1}{2}\%$ of the assumed scrap value of the plant. For example, if plant is scrapped at the end of 10 years, and the proceeds realised are 5% of the cost, the net tax saving (as a percentage of the cost) in the 11th year is -

balances of allowances remaining	1.2%
less tax at $42\frac{1}{2}\%$ on scrap value of 5%	2.1%
net saving in Year 11	-0.9%

    e.g., The balancing allowance in column 8 of Form 1 is -0.9% of £280 = approximately -£3.0.

Changes in tax rate

If there is a change in the tax rate, but no change in initial or annual allowances, the change can be accommodated by a simple modification to the tables. All the figures in the tables should be multiplied by the new rate, divided by the current rate of $42\frac{1}{2}\%$. For instance, if the rate were changed to 40%, all the figures should be multiplied by $40/42\frac{1}{2} = 0.94$.

Derivation

The following example illustrates the principle on which the table is constructed.

Plant eligible for 60% first-year allowance with 25% annual allowance thereafter, investment of £100:

	£	£
year 1 'first year' allowance		
£100 x 60%	60	
x $42\frac{1}{2}\%$ tax		25.5
year 2 annual allowance		
£(100-60) x 25%	10	
x $42\frac{1}{2}\%$ tax		4.3
- as shown in column 2 Table I		

Tax Table II

Capital Allowances on INDUSTRIAL BUILDINGS

Tax saved as a % of cost (net of grant)

tax rate $42\frac{1}{2}\%$

Number of years after purchase	Initial allowance 15% Buildings in use in:		Initial allowance 40% Buildings in use in:	
	year of purchase	year after purchase	year of purchase	year after purchase
1	8·1	6·4	18·7	17·0
2	1·7	1·7	1·7	1·7
3-15	1·7 per year	1·7 per year	1·7 per year	1·7 per year
16	1·7	1·7	-	1·7
17	1·7	1·7	-	-
18	1·7	1·7	-	-
19	1·7	1·7	-	-
20	1·7	1·7	-	-
21	1·7	1·7	-	-
22	0·4	1·7	-	-
23	-	0·4	-	-
	42·5	42·5	42·5	42·5

Note: The first two columns apply to ordinary investment areas from April 1972; the last two columns apply to development areas.

Notes to Table II (BUILDINGS)

These schedules apply under current conditions, namely -

Tax rate	$42\frac{1}{2}\%$
Initial allowance	15% or 40%
Annual allowance	4% (straight line)

To allow for changes in the tax rate see Note 6 to Table I.

The 15% initial allowance applies to ordinary locations from April 6th 1972. Until that date a 30% initial allowance applies. For a 30% initial allowance, the first-year value of tax savings is 14.5 for buildings in use in 'year of purchase' (followed by 1.7 per year until year 17), and 12·8 for 'year after purchase' (followed by 1.7 per year until year 18).

Where a building is expected to be of further use for some other purpose after a project is complete, it is recommended that it be given a residual value equal to its initial cost (net of grants) less depreciation at 4% (straight line) per year. Thus, if a building costs £100 net of any grants and comes into operation in the year after purchase, then after 10 years its residual value is £(100-(10 x 4)) = £60. This figure would be entered in column 4 of Form 1.

Where a building is expected to be of no further use at the end of a project's life, it should be given no residual value, but a balancing allowance should be claimed equal to the sum of all the remaining annual allowances. In the example quoted, there are 13 years (23 - 10) of tax life remaining, so the balancing allowance is 12 x £1.7 + £0.4 = £20.8. This should be included in the appropriate 'tax saved' column in the year after termination.

Derivation

The following examples illustrate the principles on which the table is constructed.

			£	£
(i)	In use in year of purchase			
	Year 1:	initial allowance	15	
		annual allowance	4	
			19	
		x tax at $42\frac{1}{2}\%$·		8.1
	Year 2:	annual allowance	4	
		x tax at $42\frac{1}{2}\%$		1.7
(ii)	In use in year after purchase			
	Year 1:	initial allowance	15	
		x tax at $42\frac{1}{2}\%$		6.4
	Year 2:	annual allowance	4	
		x tax at $42\frac{1}{2}\%$		1.7

Chapter 3 : Graphical Conversion from Traditional to DCF Return

I INTRODUCTION

In this section we introduce the six 'Profitability Graphs' reproduced on pages 42 to 47. The object of these is to give a rough and ready conversion from a traditional measure of profitability to a D C F return. There are separate graphs for different types of expenditure of plant, buildings, working capital and revenue expenditure. Where the project consists entirely of one category, the 'answer' can be read direct from the graph. Where the project is a mixed one, the 'answer' is obtained by taking a weighted average from the different graphs.

All the graphs assume -

(i)   all expenditure occurs in year 0

(ii) profits are constant from year 1 for the whole life of the project

(iii) Corporation Tax at the current rate of $42\frac{1}{2}\%$

(iv) that the company has sufficient profits to fully absorb the tax allowances.

Where conditions (i) and (ii) are not satisfied, adjustments can be made to allow the graphs still to be used. Changes in tax rate can be allowed for, as set out in the note on page 48.

The six graphs presented are:

A.	Plant:	60% first year allowance, 25% annual allowance thereafter
B.	Plant:	100% first year allowance
C.	Industrial Buildings:	15% initial allowance
D.	Industrial Buildings:	40% initial allowance
E.	Working Capital	
F.	Revenue Expenditure	

II USE OF PROFITABILITY GRAPHS

These graphs have been designed to be independent of the level of any grant which may be available. Thus the same graph is applicable to any Area and will continue to be applicable if the levels of investment grant are changed in the future.

It is however necessary to recognise that the grant is received a year later and that its real value is less than the nominal value. It is therefore necessary to:

<u>regard a £35 grant as worth £30</u>

<u>and a £45 grant as worth £38</u>

Simple example

Project:	all buildings (35% grant, 40% initial allowance) in a development area
Cost:	£100 gross, <u>treated as 100 - 30 = £70 net cost after grant</u>
Life:	10 years
Profit before tax:	£7.2/year constant
Depreciation:	£8.0
Cash flow:	£15.2

$$\frac{\text{Cash flow}}{\text{Net cost}} \quad = \quad \frac{15.2}{70} \quad = \quad 21.7\%$$

Using graph D, the D C F return corresponding to 21.7% on the horizontal axis and the 10 year life curve is 15%.

4. If the investment consists of a mixture of different forms of expenditure, the graphs can still be used (although some slight additional error is introduced) by taking a weighted average of the results given by the separate graphs.

Mixed example

Let us assume that the mixed project consists of the following elements.

Plant, (60% first year allowance)	£50
Buildings (15% initial allowance)	£25
Working Capital	£15
Revenue Expenditure	£10
Total Expenditure	£100
Life	10 years
Profit before tax	£16 p.a.
Depreciation	£6
Cash flow	£22
Cash flow as % of total expenditure	22%

Using graphs A, C, E and F, the D C F returns for the relevant categories had the 22% cash flow consisted solely of each of these categories, are shown as 15.6%, 14.0%, 13.8% and 17.6%. A weighted average is taken of these percentages -

Plant	15.6 x 50%	=	7.8
Buildings	14.0 x 25%	=	3.5
Working Capital	13.8 x 15%	=	2.1
Revenue Expenditure	17.6 x 10%	=	1.7
			15.1

This calculation could be done in Part 1 of Form 3, to be found at the end of this section.

III ADJUSTMENTS WHEN ALL EXPENDITURE IS NOT IN YEAR 0

In constructing the graphs, we assumed that all expenditure takes place in year 0, i.e. one year before profits start. Where this is not so in an actual project, the expenditure should be adjusted as in Part II of Form 3, to bring it onto this basis. This means applying an adjustment factor - which has been taken at a standard 10% per annum - to all expenditure occurring earlier or later than year 0, to make it equivalent to expenditure occurring in year 0. Note that year 0 is the year before the project makes its first profit or loss. Thus any expenditure taking place in year minus 1 (or 2 years before profits start) needs to be increased by 10% (i.e. multiplied by 1.1) in order to make it equivalent to money spent in year 0. This is to reflect the fact that it has been lying idle and making no contribution to profits for one year. Conversely any expenditure made in year 1 must be reduced by 10% (i.e. multiplied by 0.909) to reflect the saving involved in delaying expenditure for one year. In this way the expenditure on each category of plant, buildings, etc. is converted from the actual amount spent in any year to a notional amount spent in year 0. Also in part II of the form any grants for which the project is eligible are deducted one year after the relevant expenditure. The resulting total 'adjusted' expenditure thus represents the present value in year 0 of the total expenditure after deducting grants. Finally, the percentage division of the total adjusted expenditure between each category has to be calculated (see example on Form 3).

The graphs have been calculated on the basis that both plant and buildings come into operation in the year of purchase. Where in practice this is not the case the graphs can still be used without any adjustment. It is possible that a delay in coming into operation can affect the timing of the capital allowances, but any such influence is small enough to be ignored. This is because the first year allowance for plant and the initial allowance for buildings are given in the year in which the expenditure is incurred.

IV   ADJUSTMENT WHEN PROFITS ARE NOT CONSTANT

7.   In the assumption underlying the graphs, profits begin in year 1 and remain constant till the end of the project; accordingly if there is any variation in the profits, adjustments must be made to tailor them to this 'constant' pattern. Where the variation in profits is simple, then a quick rule can be given. For example, if the profit declines by a constant amount each year of the project's life, then (discounting at 10%) the equivalent constant annual profit is approximately:-

all figures expressed as a percentage of first year cash profit

Level of profit at end of project life	0	25	50	75
Equivalent constant annual profit	62	70	80	90

Where the profit variation is more complex the necessary adjustments require only a little calculation. This method of adjustment is shown in Part III of Form 3. The project's actual profits (before tax) are entered in column (ii) of Part III, with the first profit or loss entered against year 1, and multiplying each year's figure by the adjustment factor for that year. The total of the resultant column gives the total present value of the profits - again at 10% discount. This total must then be multiplied by the conversion factor corresponding to the last year of the project. This gives the figure we are seeking: the notional profit the project would need to earn each year if its profits were constant instead of variable. For example, if the total of the resultant column is £100, and the project has a 12-year life (i.e. conversion factor = 0.147) the actual profits can be said to be equivalent to £14.7 each year for years 1 - 12.

V   WORKED EXAMPLE

To illustrate the arithmetic - which is a lot simpler than a verbal presentation makes it sound - we show in Form 3 an estimate for the example in Chapter 2. There, using the full method of Forms 1 and 2 and the Interpolation Chart, we derived the solution of 11% D C F. Here in Form 3, we estimate, more quickly, an approximate answer of 10.8%.

FORM 3

STANDARD FORM FOR USE WITH PROFITABILITY GRAPHS

Project	Nature of project: *Expansion of lawn-mower plant (as example in chapter 2)*	
	Total Expenditure - gross cost	*£ 795,000*
	- net cost after deducting grants	
	Profit, at peak - after depreciation, before tax	*£ 175,000*
	Return on capital (net cost)	*22%*
	D C F Return (implicitly after tax)	*10.8% **

Part I   Calculation of D C F Return

	£ '000
Profits, after depreciation, on a constant basis (from Part III if adjustment necessary)	*79.4*
Depreciation* (if not already included above)	*55*
PROFITS BEFORE DEPRECIATION	*134.4*
Expenditure (adjusted - from Part II)	*757*
Profit before Depreciation as % of Expenditure	*17.7%*

	D C F Return from Graph	Weighting (From II)	Resultant Returns %
Plant - 60% first year allowance	*10.7*	*61%*	*6.5%*
Plant - 100% first year allowance	*-*	*-*	*-*
Buildings - 15% initial allowance	*10.7*	*22.4%*	*2.4%*
Buildings - 40% initial allowance	*-*	*-*	*-*
Working Capital	*11.1*	*14%*	*1.6%*
Revenue Expenditure	*12.0*	*2.6%*	*0.3%*
Total		*100%*	*10.8% ***

* which must be on a straight-line basis

Part II   Adjustment of Expenditure, if not all in Year 0 (and deduction of grants)

£ '000

Year	Adjustment factor	PLANT				BUILDINGS					Working Capital		R Exp
		60% first year allowance		100% first year allowance		15% initial allowance		40% initial allowance					
		Actual	Adjusted	Actual	Adjusted	Actual	Adjusted	Actual	Grant	Adjusted	Actual	Adjusted	Actual
-3	1·33												
-2	1·21												
-1	1·1												
0*	1·0	*280*	*280*			*170*	*170*						*20*
1	0·909	*200*	*182*								*50*	*45*	
2	0·826										*50*	*41*	
3	0·751										*25*	*19*	
TOTALS		*480*	*462*			*170*	*170*				*125*	*105*	*20*
% division of adjusted Total			*61%*				*22.4%*					*14%*	

* one year before first profits are earned (or loss sustained)

Part III

Adjustments to profits (either before or after depreciation) if not constant

Year (i)	Actual Profit £'000 (ii)	Adjustment Factor (iii)	Resultant (iv)	Conversion Factor* (v)
1	(-90)	0·909	(-82)	1·1
2	10	0·826	8	0·576
3	115	0·751	86	0·402
4	175	0·683 ⎤		0·315
5	175	0·621 ⎬ 1.868	327	0·264
6	175	0·564 ⎦		0·230
7	145	0·513	74	0·205
8	95	0·467	44	0·187
9	65	0·424	28	0·174
10	5	0·386	2	0·163
11		0·350		0·154
12		0·319		0·147
13		0·290		0·141
14		0·263		0·136
15		0·239		0·131
16		0·218		0·128
17		0·198		0·125
18		0·180		0·122
19		0·164		0·120
20		0·149		0·117
	Total		487	£'000

x conversion factor for last year of profit 0.163 = equivalent constant annual profit of 79.4

* the factor is the 'number of £ needed to be earned each year to give a 10% return on £1 invested in year 0'. It is in fact the annuity that could be bought for £1 at 10% interest.

** This 10.8% compares well with the 11% derived by the lengthier and more accurate method of chapter 2.

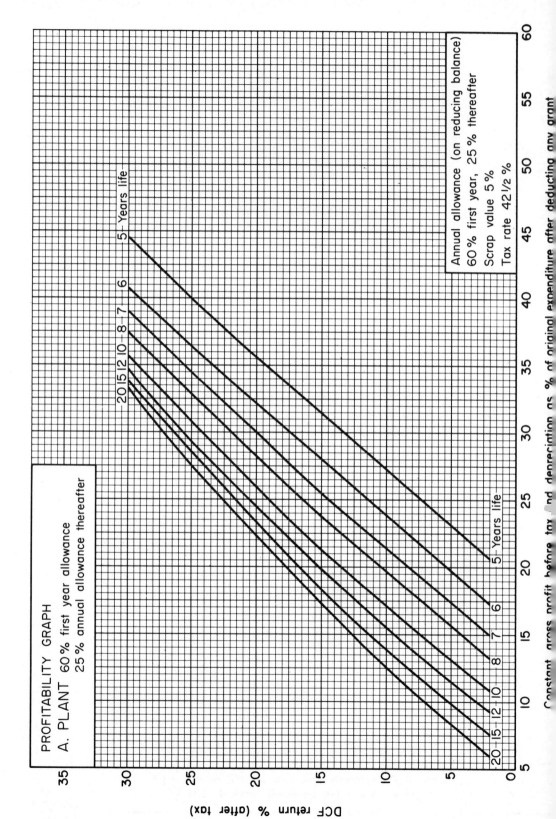

PROFITABILITY GRAPH
A. PLANT 60% first year allowance
25% annual allowance thereafter

Annual allowance (on reducing balance)
60% first year, 25% thereafter
Scrap value 5%
Tax rate 42½%

DCF return % (after tax)

Constant gross profit before tax and depreciation as % of original expenditure after deducting any grant

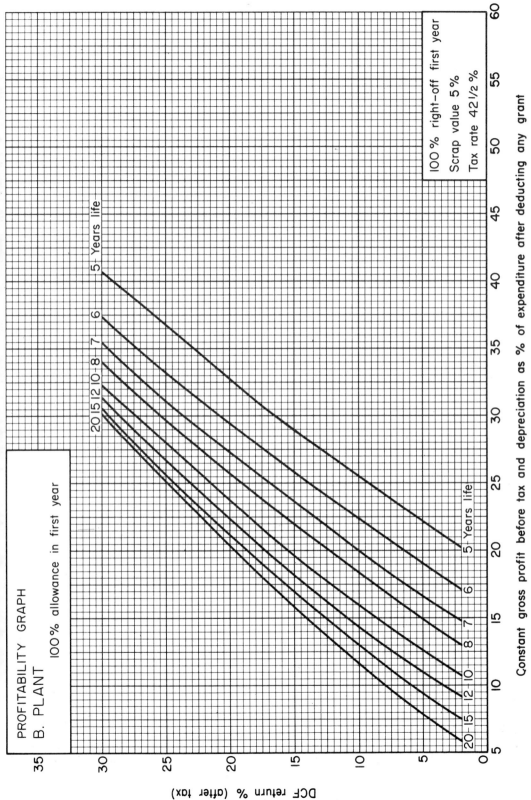

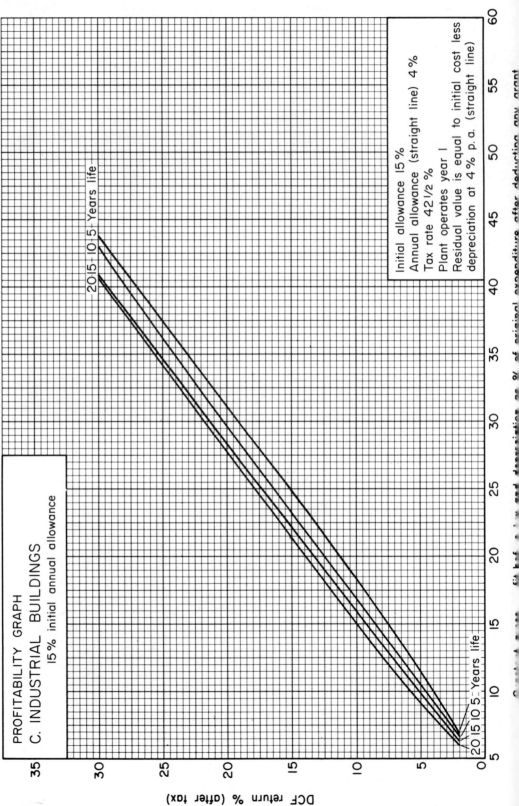

PROFITABILITY GRAPH
C. INDUSTRIAL BUILDINGS
15% initial annual allowance

Initial allowance 15%
Annual allowance (straight line) 4%
Tax rate 42½%
Plant operates year I
Residual value is equal to initial cost less
depreciation at 4% p.a. (straight line)

DCF return % (after tax)

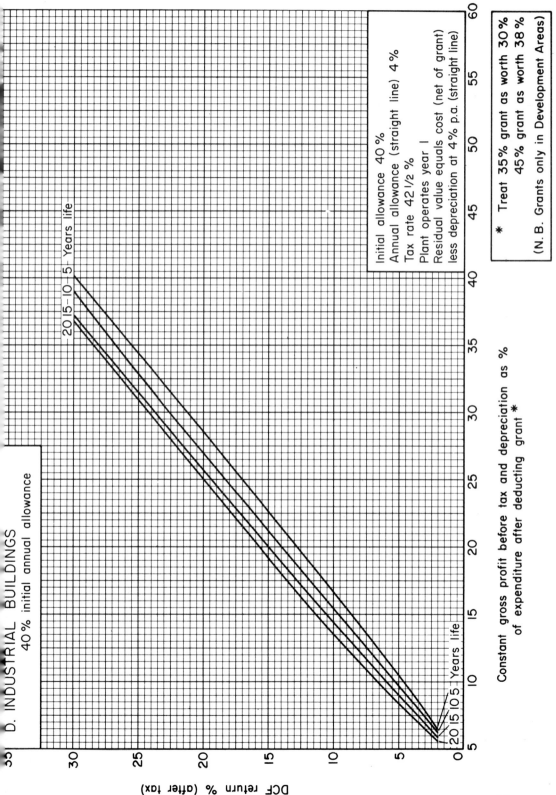

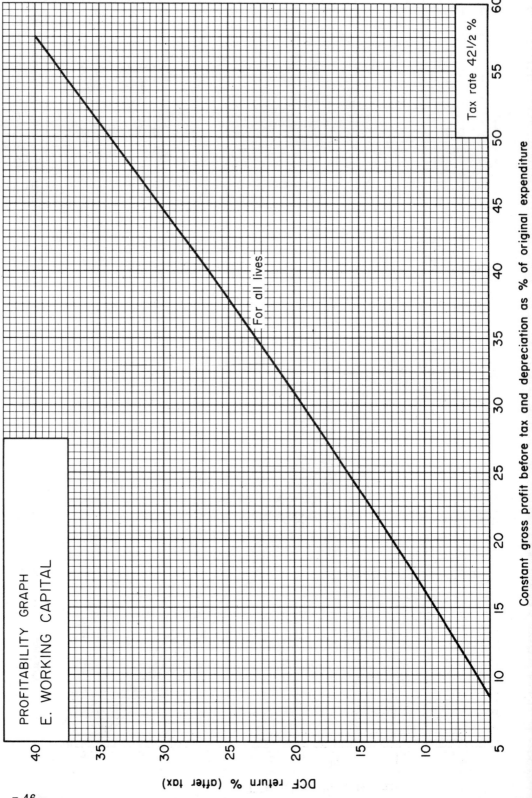

PROFITABILITY GRAPH
E. WORKING CAPITAL

For all lives

Tax rate 42½ %

DCF return % (after tax)

Constant gross profit before tax and depreciation as % of original expenditure

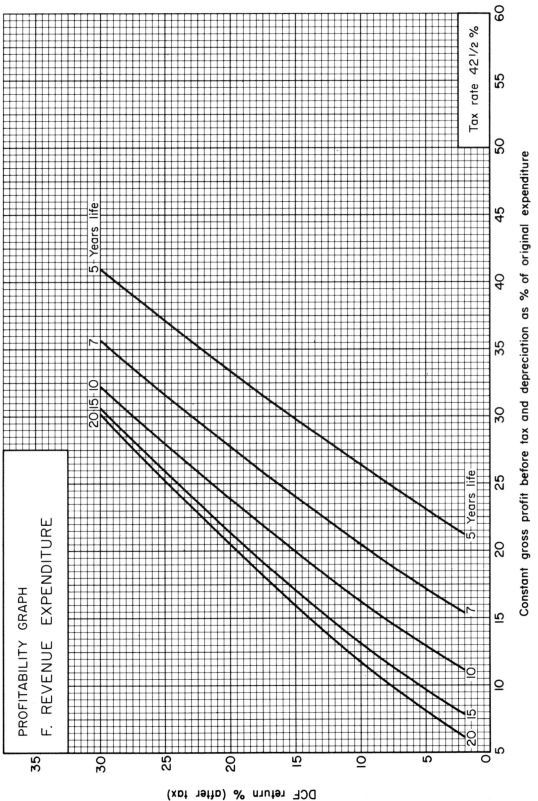

PROFITABILITY GRAPH
F. REVENUE EXPENDITURE

Tax rate 42½ %

5- Years life

7

20 15 10

5- Years life

7

10

20 15

DCF return % (after tax)

Constant gross profit before tax and depreciation as % of original expenditure

CHAPTER 3 : METHOD WITH PROFITABILITY GRAPHS

ADJUSTMENTS TO PROFITABILITY GRAPHS

(a) <u>Buildings eligible for 30% initial allowance</u>

In Ordinary locations, buildings will be eligible for a 30% initial allowance until
April 5th 1972. This graph has been omitted. Data can, however, be derived by
calculating the D C F returns on the basis of a 15% initial allowance and <u>adding</u> the
following amounts:

Where D C F return on 15% Initial Allowance is	Add the following to give the D C F return for 30% Initial Allowance
5%	$\frac{1}{2}\%$
10%	$\frac{3}{4}\%$
15%	1%
20%	$1\frac{1}{4}\%$

(b) <u>If Corporation Tax falls by 5% (i.e. to 37½%)</u>

A lower Corporation Tax will increase the D C F return on investments (and a higher
rate will decrease it). For a 5% <u>reduction</u> in Corporation Tax <u>increase</u> the readings
from the graphs by the following amounts:

For a life of (years)	At an original D C F return of:		
	5%	10%	15%
PLANT: 60% first-year allowance			
5	0·1	0·5	0·5
10 or more	0·2	0·2	0·3
PLANT: 100% first-year allowance			
5	0·4	0·3	0·0
10 or more	0·3	0·0	0·0
INDUSTRIAL BUILDINGS: 15% initial allowance			
5	0·5	1·0	1·2
10 or more	0·2	0·6	1·0
INDUSTRIAL BUILDINGS: 40% initial allowance			
5	0·3	0·8	0·8
10 or more	0·5	0·6	0·8

<u>Working Capital.</u> A 5% lower Corporation Tax would <u>increase</u> the D C F return
(as read from the graph) by about one-thirteenth, e.g. 13% D C F becomes 14% D C F.

<u>Revenue Expenditure.</u> No adjustment is necessary.

Chapter 4 : Short Cut Method using
Capital Allowance Graphs

I INTRODUCTION

Chapter 2 described in detail the full-scale method of doing D C F calculations, whereby all the elements of the cash flow are added to give annual totals, each total then being discounted separately. Chapter 3 gave a short cut method involving Profitability Graphs, which give fairly accurate answers under the somewhat restrictive conditions of constant gross profit and all expenditure in one year, and approximate answers where the investment can be adjusted to comply with these conditions. There discounting was dispensed with completely, except as part of the adjustment process.

The method in the present Chapter combines the accuracy of the first method with the brevity of the second. We have already noted that one of the chief bugbears to the arithmetic of D C F is the irregularity of the pattern of tax savings on capital allowances, which in turn makes for irregularity in the total net cash flow figures of any project, whether the profits are relatively constant or not. A convenient way round this is to divide the cash inflow into its two main components: tax savings, and profits after tax. If the discounted (or present) value of the former can be given in a convenient, ready-made form, which also includes typical residual values of plant and buildings, all that remains is to discount the profits and (in one calculation) deduct tax; and there are various simplified ways of discounting different patterns of profit.

II CAPITAL ALLOWANCE GRAPHS

At the end of the Chapter we include four capital allowance graphs, namely:

A	Plant	:	60% first year allowance
B	"	:	100% first year allowance
C	Industrial buildings*	:	15% initial allowance
D	" "	:	40% " "

The precise assumptions on which they are based include –
  (i)   Corporation Tax @ $42\frac{1}{2}\%$
  (ii) Scrap value at 5% for plant
  (iii) Residual value on buildings equal to the expenditure (net of grant) less depreciation at 4% (straight line) per year.
  (iv) The company has sufficient profits to absorb the tax allowances in full. .

* Adjustment factor for buildings with 30% initial allowance is given on page 61.

What the graphs show is simply the percentage of the investment, after deducting any grant, that is recovered in tax savings and residual values, after discounting at any rate of discount. This is given for a range of different lives. For example, suppose we wish to calculate the value at 10% discount of the capital allowances (together with the scrap value) on £100 of investment in plant eligible for 60% first year allowance and 25% annual allowances thereafter, which has a 10 year life. Graph A shows that for £100 of such investment the allowances at 10% discount are worth £35.6. On a similar investment made in buildings (with 15% initial allowance and no grant), the recovery (capital allowances and residual value) can be taken straight from the graph and at 10% is £36.4.

III SOME SHORT CUTS IN DISCOUNTING PROFITS

(a) Constant Profits

4.   The first simple rule is based on the fact that, for example, £100 earns 10% D C F if it earns £10/year indefinitely. Put another way, the present value of £10/year indefinitely at 10% discount is £100. More generally, where a constant sum of money is received each year for an indefinite period, its present value is that sum divided by the discount rate. For example, a sum of £10 received for an indefinite period is worth:

at 10% discount: £10/0.1 = £100   at 20% discount: £10/0.2 = £50

5.   Where a constant sum is received for a limited period, its present value could be derived by multiplying it by the series of annual discount factors. For example, £10 a year for 10 years at 15% discount would be:

$$£10 \text{ x } 0.870 \text{ (year 1)}$$
$$\text{plus } £10 \text{ x } 0.756 \text{ (year 2)}$$
$$\text{etc.}$$

Much quicker is to multiply it by the <u>sum</u> of the discount factors for the years 1-10. These can be found in Interest Table B in Chapter 5. The 15% column shows that the sum after two years (0.870 plus 0.756) is 1.626 and after ten years 5.019. So £10 for 10 years at 15% discount is worth (or has a present value of) £50.19.

6.   A further simple device helps in adjusting profits for tax payments. As tax is normally paid about 1 year after the profits are earned, the effective tax rate is not, say $42\frac{1}{2}\%$, but

$42\frac{1}{2}\%$ discounted for 1 year at the relevant rate of discount, i.e. the solution rate for the project concerned. As the tax proportion is constant over the years, tax can be deducted in one calculation from the present value of the profits (effective tax rates are given on page 56, and are applied in the following example).

Example: all plant constant profits (the project of Appendix B in Chapter 1)

Investment	£100
Traditional profit	£7.0 p.a.
Depreciation	£10.0 p.a.
Gross profit	£17.0 p.a.
Life	10 years

Let us assume we do not know the answer, and so try discount rates of 9% and 11%. We then have:

		Discounted at		
		9%		11%
		£		£
Cash Outflow				
Investment (A)		100		100
Cash Inflow				
Present value of capital allowances and scrap		36.4		35.0
Annual profit of £17.0 x sum of discount factors for years 1-10 (from Interest Table B)				
@ 9% discount (6.418)		109.0		
@ 11% discount (5.889)				100.0
		145.4		135
less tax at $42\frac{1}{2}\%$ on profits lagged one year	(39.0%)	42.5	(38.3%)	38.3
Present value of cash inflow (B)		102.9		96.7
Outflow/Inflow (A/B)		0.97		1.03

CHAPTER 4 : SECOND SHORT CUT METHOD

By interpolation to find the discount rate at which the discounted values of outflow and inflow are equal (i. e. A/B = 1.0), it can be seen that the D C F return is 10%, the same answer as that derived in Appendix B to Chapter 1.

If profits are not strictly constant, but for example were profits of £20 for years 1 to 5 and £10 for years 6 to 10 their present value at 9% discount is given from data in Table B as

$$£20 \times 3.890 = 77.80$$
$$£10 \times 2.528 = 25.28$$
$$\overline{103.08}$$

The figure of 2.528 is simply the value for 10 years (6.418) less the value for 5 years (3.890).

(b) Profits rising or declining at a constant rate

8. Where profits are expected to change at a constant rate, for an indefinite period, their present value can be found by the expedient of altering the discount rate. Thus if one expects to receive an income of £100 in year 1, rising by 5% a year compound indefinitely, its present value at 15% discount is £100/0.15-0.05 = £100/0.1 = £1,000. If the income is declining at 5% a year from year 2 onwards, its present value would be £100/0.15 + 0.05 = £100/0.2 = £500. To apply this simple expedient when the period of the investment is limited, a reasonably close answer (especially for long lives) is given by exactly the same method, e.g. £100 in year 1, declining by 5% a year from year 2 until year 15, and discounted at 15% can, as an approximation, be taken as equivalent to a constant income of £100 per year discounted at 20% (15% plus 5%). Using the 20% rate gives an answer (from Interest Table B, 20% column, year 15) of £468 instead of the real answer of £472, i. e. an under-statement of about 1%. In all cases where there is an annual decline in profits, this short method will slightly understate the present value of profits, and hence will understate the D C F rate of return. Where the annual profits are increasing the present value and the D C F return will be slightly overstated. In all normal cases, the error will not exceed ½% D C F.

Example: all plant (60% first year allowance, 25% annual allowance): cost £100

Profit: Year 1   :   £22

declining by 5% compound to £13.8 in year 10.

Selecting 10% and 15% as our trial discount rates, we have:

	Discounted at	
	10%	15%
Cash Outflow	£	£
Investment (A)	100	100

Cash inflow		Discounted at	
		10%	15%
Capital allowances (£100 x graph A)		35.6	32.5
Gross profits (treated as a constant £22) using Interest Table B and discounting:			
@ 10% + 5% = 15%		110.4	
@ 15% + 5% = 20%			92.2
		146.0	124.7
less tax at 42½% lagged 1 year	(38.6%)	42.6 (39.0%)	34.1
Present value of cash inflow (B)		103.4	90.6
A/B		0.97	1.12

By interpolation to find the discount rate at which A/B = 1, we find it is 11.2%. This understates the true result by 0.4%.

(c) Short life with varying cash flow

In cases of shorter lives, or where more accurate results are required, the profits need to be discounted year by year.

Example   Investment: plant £100

Life: 5 years

Profit: £45 declining to £10 as shown

		Discounted at	
		5%	10%
Cash Outflow		£	£
Investment (A)		100	100

Cash Inflow

Year	Expected Gross Profits		
1	45	42.8	40.9
2	35	31.7	28.9
3	20	17.3	15.0
4	10	8.2	6.8
5	10	7.8	6.2
		107.8	97.8
less tax 42½% lagged 1 year	(40.5%)	43.6 (38.6%)	37.8
		64.6	60.0
Capital allowances (£100 x Graph A)		40.6	36.8
Present value of cash inflow (B)		105.2	96.8
A/B		0.95	1.03

Since the D C F solution rate is the one at which the cash outflow and inflow are equal, it can be seen by interpolation to be roughly 8%.

(d) Application to a complex example

10. The examples so far are for special cases. But this method can also be used for the more complex projects. As an example, we take the project examined by the 'full' method in Chapter 2, (and by the 'Profitability Graph' method in Chapter 3).

11. If we did not know the D C F return we would, of course, have to find it by trial and error. Here, as we are seeking to establish the principle only we are showing just one set of calculations, i.e. at the solution rate of 11%.

12. Investment and Profit; details as on page 64.

CASH OUTFLOW*

	Actual Expenditure £'000	Discount factors at 11%	Discounted Cash Outflow £'000
Year 0	470	1.0	470
1	250	0.901	226
2	50	0.812	41
3	25	0.731	18
		total	755

CASH INFLOW

Cash Recoveries on Plant (see graph A)   £'000

  10 year life: 34.8% x 280   97

  9 year life: 34.9% x 200 x 0.901 **   63

                                                              160

---

* The treatment of the cash outflow is merely an abbreviated version of the procedure followed on Forms 1 and 2 (Chapter 2).

** The 9 year life plant is purchased in Year 1; the value of the capital allowances is therefore discounted to year 0.

Cash Recoveries on Buildings (see graph C)

    10 year life: 33% x 170   56

Tax Saving on Revenue Expenditure

    $42\frac{1}{2}$% x 20 x 0.901 (i.e. lagged one year)   8

Recovery of Working Capital

    125 x 0.352 * (in year 10 of project)   44

Profits before tax and depreciation

	Profit £'000	Discount factor, at 11%	Discounted £'000
Year 1	(-35)	0.901	(-32)
2	65	0.812	53
3	170	0.731	124
4-6	230	1.787	411
7	200	0.482	96
8	150	0.434	65
9	120	0.391	47
10	60	0.352	21
			785
less tax at $42\frac{1}{2}$% lagged 1 year (38.3%)			300
			485

SUMMARY   £'000

Total cash outflow (discounted at 11%)   755

Total cash inflow (discounted at 11%)

plant	160
buildings	56
revenue expenditure	8
working capital	44
profits after tax	485
total	753

As outflow approximately equals inflow, the D C F return = 11%

* Discount factor at 11% for year 10.

CHAPTER 4 : SECOND SHORT CUT METHOD

Normally all the above calculations would be done for 2 or more "guessed" D C F returns, and the final result determined by interpolation. This method probably halves the time taken by the full method of Chapter 2.

APPENDIX

TAX RATES DISCOUNTED FOR ONE YEAR

Discount Rate	Tax Rate			Discount Rate	Tax Rate		
	35%	40%	45%		35%	40%	45%
1%	34.6	39.6	44.6	14%	30.7	35.1	39.5
2%	34.3	39.2	44.1	15%	30.4	34.8	39.2
3%	34.0	38.8	43.7	16%	30.2	34.5	38.8
4%	33.7	38.5	43.3	17%	29.9	34.2	38.4
5%	33.3	38.1	42.8	18%	29.6	33.9	38.1
6%	33.0	37.7	42.4	19%	29.4	33.6	37.8
7%	32.7	37.4	42.1	20%	29.2	33.3	37.5
8%	32.4	37.0	41.7				
9%	32.1	36.7	41.3	25%	28.0	32.0	36.0
10%	31.8	36.4	40.9	30%	26.9	30.8	34.6
11%	31.5	36.0	40.5	35%	25.9	29.6	33.3
12%	31.3	35.7	40.2	40%	25.0	28.6	32.1
13%	31.0	35.4	39.8				

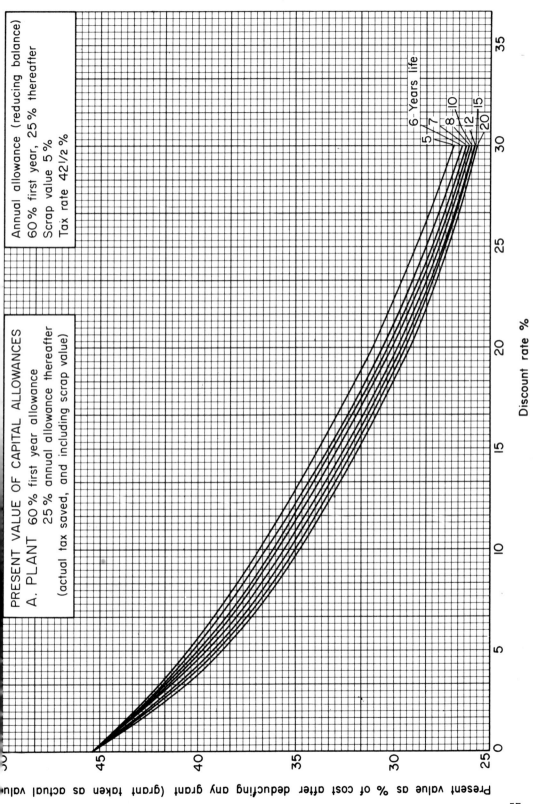

PRESENT VALUE OF CAPITAL ALLOWANCES

A. PLANT   60% first year allowance
            25% annual allowance thereafter
            (actual tax saved, and including scrap value)

Annual allowance (reducing balance)
60% first year, 25% thereafter
Scrap value 5%
Tax rate 42½%

6 Years life
5
7
8
10
12
15
20

Discount rate %

Present value as % of cost after deducting any grant (grant taken as actual value)

= 57 =

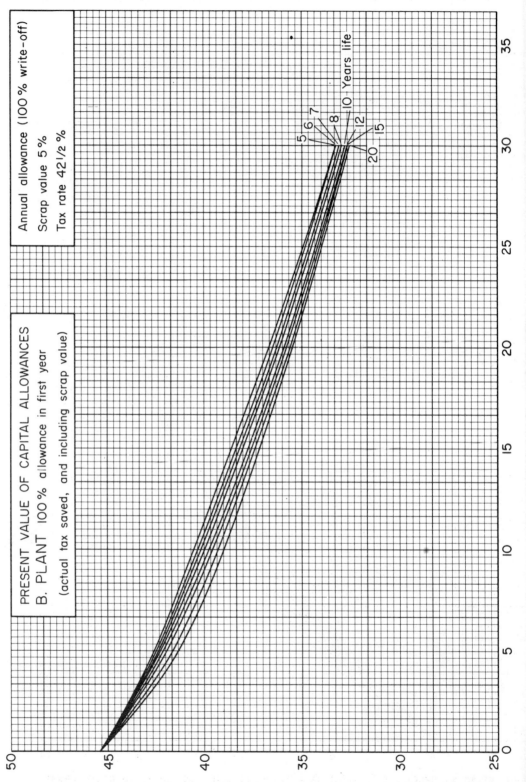

PRESENT VALUE OF CAPITAL ALLOWANCES
B. PLANT 100 % allowance in first year
(actual tax saved, and including scrap value)

Annual allowance (I00 % write-off)
Scrap value 5 %
Tax rate 4 I/2 %

Present value as % of cost after deducting any grant (grant taken as actual value)

= 58 =

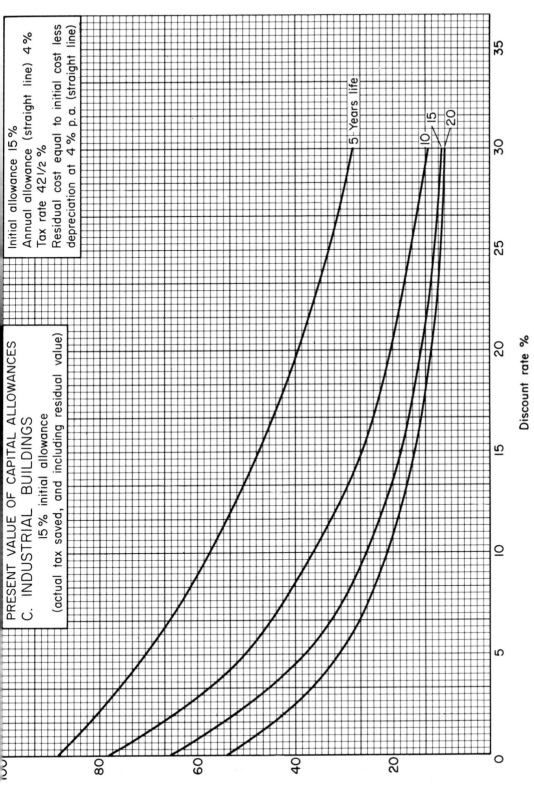

PRESENT VALUE OF CAPITAL ALLOWANCES
C. INDUSTRIAL BUILDINGS
15% initial allowance
(actual tax saved, and including residual value)

Initial allowance 15%
Annual allowance (straight line) 4%
Tax rate 42½%
Residual cost equal to initial cost less depreciation at 4% p.a. (straight line)

Discount rate %

Present value as % of cost after deducting any grant (grant taken as actual value)

= 59 =

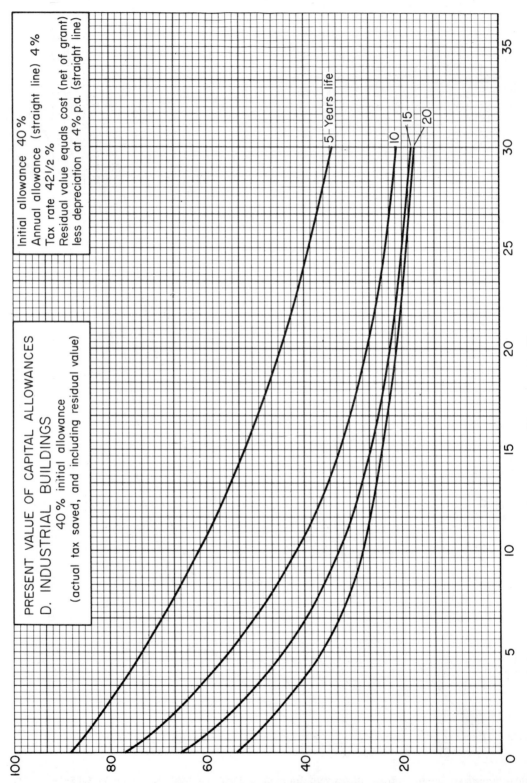

ADJUSTMENTS TO CAPITAL ALLOWANCE GRAPHS

Buildings eligible for 30% initial allowance

In ordinary locations, buildings will be eligible for 30% initial allowance until April 5, 1972. Data for this situation can easily be obtained by interpolating between the graphs C and D. The rule is, to the reading from graph C (i. e. 15% initial allowance) add three-fifths of the difference between the readings from graphs C and D. For example, for a building with a 10-year project life, and for 10% discount, the present value of the capital allowance plus residual value is

at 15% initial allowance	36. 4
at 40% initial allowance	41. 8

Three fifths of the difference is 3. 3, therefore

at 30% initial allowance	39. 7

Change in tax rates

For plant, a rough adjustment (which will normally be sufficient for all practical purposes) can be made by multiplying the figures on the graphs by the new tax rate and dividing by the old. For example, if the new tax rate is 40%, all the readings are multiplied by $\frac{40}{42.5} = 0.94$. The adjustment is rough becuase the graphs contain the scrap value, which is not dependent on the tax rate. But only for very short lives, or very large changes in tax rates, will the error be significant (in which case it can be avoided by subtracting the (discounted) scrap value before adjusting, and then adding it back.)

For buildings residual values (which do not depend on the tax rate) are large, but adjusment is relatively easy because the annual allowances are calculated by the straight-line method, and their present value can therefore be quickly recalculated. The easiest method is simply to calculate the difference in present value caused by the tax change, and add or subtract this to the appropriate reading from the graph.

For example, suppose the tax rate decreases by 5% to $37\frac{1}{2}\%$, and we are considering buildings to be used in an ordinary location for 10 years at 10% discount, and costing £100.

CHAPTER 4 : SECOND SHORT CUT METHOD

We have:

	Gross value of allowances	Tax at 5%	Discount factors at 10%	Present value
Year 1	15*	0.75	0.909	0.7
Years 2-10	4*	0.2	5.236	1.0
Year 11	(-11)**	0.55	0.35	0.2
				1.9

Subtracting the answer from the reading of 36·6 on the graph C gives an equivalent answer of 34·7% with a $37\frac{1}{2}\%$ tax rate.

* Initial allowance of 15% in year 1; annual allowance of 4% per annum (straight-line).

** Balancing item: the residual value is £60 (£100 less depreciation at £4 per year for 10 years), and the tax written down value is £49 (£100 less £15 initial allowance less £4 per year for nine years); the resultant is a (negative) balancing item of -11.

Chapter 5 : Reference Material

1.	COMPANY/DIVISION		Reference *LMD. 16/70*
	Manufacturing		Date *October 1970*

2. TITLE OF PROJECT

Expansion of High Wycombe Plant

3. REASON FOR RECOMMENDING PROJECT (with covering note if necessary)

To increase capacity to produce high quality lawn mowers, and enable the company to keep its share of this growing and profitable market.

4. WHETHER INCLUDED IN FORECAST SUBMITTED IN 1969

Yes

5.	COST OF PROJECT	£'000
	Plant (before deducting grants)	436
	Buildings (before deducting grants)	155
	Allied revenue expenditure	18
	Working capital	125
	Contingency	61 ✝✱
	(Less realisations from assets scrapped)	(—)
	TOTAL FOR WHICH APPROVAL NOW SOUGHT	795
	Less Grants receivable	
	Net Expenditure	795

6.	PROFIT OR SAVING AT PEAK (most likely assumptions)	£'000
	for **3** years from 19**74** to 19**76**)✝	175

7. PROFITABILITY	most likely assumptions	alternative assumptions	
		"worse"	"better"
D C F Return (after tax*)	11.0 %	7.8 %	14.6 %
Traditional Return at peak (as % of expenditure less grants)	22.0 %		
Pay-back (after tax)	5 ✝ years		
Profit as % of Turnover (at peak)	17 %		

* after taking account of any further expenditure under item 10.

✱✱ *divided among plant, buildings etc. in item 13.*

✝ *in this example, in the interests of simplicity in presentation, the possible change in profits from rising real wages is ignored.*

✝ *number of years before the cash flow in column 7 of FORM 2 repays the investment, excluding working capital.*

8. THE EXTENT TO WHICH ALTERNATIVES HAVE BEEN CONSIDERED

The possibility of siting the extra plant at our factory in Cornwall was considered, but additional transport costs to our main distribution centres makes this uneconomical.

9. UNDERLYING ASSUMPTIONS (price and costs relative to present levels, % capacity working, life)

(a) most likely

Capacity working
1971   30%
1972   60%
1973   80%
1974   90%

Prices: at current levels till 1975.
Costs: variable costs at current levels till 1975.
Profits have been reduced from 1976 to allow for higher costs or lower prices thereafter.

(b) possible variations ("better" and "worse")

better: 100% capacity working from 1975 onwards.
worse: prices lower by 5% from 1975 onwards.

10. PROBABLE FURTHER EXPENDITURE DURING LIFE OF PROJECT
to maintain forecast profits (estimate, with explanations necessary)

None: an adequate provision for repairs and maintenance has been allowed for.

11. COMMITMENTS ALREADY MADE

None.

12. IS THIS PROJECT PART OF A LARGER SCHEME? (if so, give details)

The components division may expand its factory in due course to meet the increased demand, but have not yet done a profitability study. This project has been costed on the basis of bought-in components.

13. RATES OF EXPENDITURE (N.B. contingency to be allocated between items)

	1970	1971	1972	TOTAL
	£ '000			
Plant (before deducting grants)	280	200		480
Buildings (before deducting grants)	170			170
Allied revenue *	20			20
Working capital +		50	75(a)	125
(Less realisation from assets scrapped)	( )	( )	( )	(–)
TOTAL INCLUDING CONTINGENCY (before deducting grants)	470	250	75(a)	

TOTAL FOR WHICH APPROVAL NOW SOUGHT 795

(a) £25,000 in 1973

Current value, if any, of existing surplus assets to be used:

* including running in costs

+ net increase after deducting any associated reductions

= 65 =

14. CASH FLOW SCHEDULE (to be completed for first five years, unless payback period longer) on most likely assumptions.

		OUTFLOW		INFLOW	NET CASH FLOW
	Cost of Project	Grants Receivable	Net Expenditure	Cash Profits less Net Tax Payments	
			£'000		
1970	470		470		(-470)
1971	250		250	56	(-194)
1972	50		50	146	96
1973	25		25	163	138
1974				174	174
1975				175	145
19					
19					

15. REVENUE AND COSTS (on "most likely" assumptions at peak)

	£'000	%
SALES – Annual sales or value of production arising directly from this project (at peak)	1030	100
COSTS – Related costs of production, marketing and distribution		
– VARIABLE 380		37
– DEPRECIATION 55		5
– OTHER FIXED COSTS 420		41
– TOTAL	855	83
PROFIT – At peak	175	17

16. ESTIMATED COMPLETION DATE

December 1970

17. DATE APPROVED BY DIVISIONAL BOARD

June 1969

18. OFFICIALS RESPONSIBLE FOR PREPARING AND EXAMINING APPLICATION

Sales Director
Production Director
Chief Engineer
Chief Accountant

Submitted by:
Managing Director

BIBLIOGRAPHY

Books or Booklets

1. A comprehensive book covering all aspects of the principles of the subject.
   The only British book of its type.

   'The Finance and Analysis of Capital Projects'
   by A.J. Merrett and Allen Sykes.
   Longmans, 1962; 544 pages, 45/-

2. A shorter and simpler book, but written in the U.S.A.

   'The Capital Budgeting Decision'
   by Harold Bierman Jnr and Seymour Smidt.
   The Macmillan Co., New York 1960;
   241 pages, 42/- (in U.K.)

3. An even shorter book, concentrating on practical examples written in Australia

   'The Economics of Capital Expenditure'
   by K.A. Middleton

   with special section on 'The Replacement Problem'

   by F.K. Wright
   Australian Society of Accounts; Revised
   Edition 1964; 64 pages, $1 (Australian)

4. A booklet by N.E.D.C. urging more rational investment criteria

   'Investment Appraisal' - May 1965 - 14 pages, 1/9
   (to be re-issued shortly)

5. The practical counterpart of 1 (with special emphasis on replacement)

   'Capital Budgeting & Company Finance'
   by A.J. Merrett and Allen Sykes.
   Longmans, 1966; 184 pages, 20/-

Articles

6. An introductory pamphlet to D C F

   'Discounted Cash Flow and Corporate Planning'
   Woolwich Economic Papers No. 3 by
   A.M. Alfred, Woolwich Polytechnic, S.E.18.
   1st published July 1964: 22 pages, 3/6

7. The basic reference to historical yields on equity capital

   'Return on Equities and Fixed Interest Securities
   1919-1963'
   District Bank Review, December 1963 by
   A.J. Merrett and Allen Sykes

Examples of application of D C F to unusual circumstances

8. 'Investment in the Development Districts of the United Kingdom: Tax and Discounted Cash Flow'
Journal of Accounting Research, Vol. 2, No. 2, Autumn 1964, by A.M. Alfred

9. 'The Corporation Tax and the Incentive to Invest'
Investment Analyst No. 10 - December 1964 by A.M. Alfred and J.B. Evans

10. 'The New Investment Incentives'
The Investment Analyst
No. 14, May 1966, by Harold Rose

CAPITAL ALLOWANCES AND INVESTMENT GRANTS

Listed below are the rate of capital allowances and investment grants announced in October 1970 (for full details see the White Paper "Investment Incentives" - Cmnd. 4516, October 1970).

GENERAL	First-Year Allowance (Plant) or Initial Allowance (Buildings)	Annual Allowance
	%	%
A. PLANT		
(a) Ordinary location	60	25 (reducing balance)
(b) Development area	100% write off	
Second-hand plant in all areas	60	25 (reducing balance)
B. BUILDINGS New industrial buildings and structures		
(a) Ordinary location		
until April 5 1972	30	4 (straight-line)
from April 6 1972	15	4 (" ")
(b) Development area and Intermediate area	40	4 (" ")

GRANTS are available for new industrial buildings in Development areas at a rate of 35% (and 45% in special cases), and in Intermediate areas at a rate of 25% (and 35% in special cases).

SPECIAL ITEMS	First-Year Allowance	Annual Allowance
	%	%
A. SHIPS	100% write off	
B. VEHICLES		
Private cars (unless used in car hire or taxi business)	25	25
Commercials	60	25
C. PLANT for Scientific Research	100% write off	

Note: Initial allowances and other depreciation provisions are calculated on the cost of the asset after deducting any grant.

INTEREST TABLE A

PRESENT VALUE OF £1

(Assuming that the £1 is received in a single payment on the last day of the year)

Years Hence	1%	2%	3%	4%	5%	6%	7%	8%	9%	10%	11%	12%	13%	14%	15%	Years Hence
1	.990	.980	.971	.962	.952	.943	.935	.926	.917	.909	.901	.893	.885	.877	.870	1
2	.980	.961	.943	.925	.907	.890	.873	.857	.842	.826	.812	.797	.783	.769	.756	2
3	.971	.942	.915	.889	.864	.840	.816	.794	.772	.751	.731	.712	.693	.675	.658	3
4	.961	.924	.888	.855	.823	.792	.763	.735	.708	.683	.659	.636	.613	.592	.572	4
5	.951	.906	.863	.822	.784	.747	.713	.681	.650	.621	.593	.567	.543	.519	.497	5
6	.942	.888	.837	.790	.746	.705	.666	.630	.596	.564	.535	.507	.480	.456	.432	6
7	.933	.871	.813	.760	.711	.665	.623	.583	.547	.513	.482	.452	.425	.400	.376	7
8	.923	.853	.789	.731	.677	.627	.582	.540	.502	.467	.434	.404	.376	.351	.327	8
9	.914	.837	.766	.703	.645	.592	.544	.500	.460	.424	.391	.361	.333	.308	.284	9
10	.905	.820	.744	.676	.614	.558	.508	.463	.422	.386	.352	.322	.295	.270	.247	10
11	.896	.804	.722	.650	.585	.527	.475	.429	.388	.350	.317	.287	.261	.237	.215	11
12	.887	.788	.701	.625	.557	.497	.444	.397	.356	.319	.286	.257	.231	.208	.187	12
13	.879	.773	.681	.601	.530	.469	.415	.368	.326	.290	.258	.229	.204	.182	.163	13
14	.870	.758	.661	.577	.505	.442	.388	.340	.299	.263	.232	.205	.181	.160	.141	14
15	.861	.743	.642	.555	.481	.417	.362	.315	.275	.239	.209	.183	.160	.140	.123	15
16	.853	.728	.623	.534	.458	.394	.339	.292	.252	.218	.188	.163	.141	.123	.107	16
17	.844	.714	.605	.513	.436	.371	.317	.270	.231	.198	.170	.146	.125	.108	.093	17
18	.836	.700	.587	.494	.416	.350	.296	.250	.212	.180	.153	.130	.111	.095	.081	18
19	.828	.686	.570	.475	.396	.331	.277	.232	.194	.164	.138	.116	.098	.083	.070	19
20	.820	.673	.554	.456	.377	.312	.258	.215	.178	.149	.124	.104	.087	.073	.061	20
21	.811	.660	.538	.439	.359	.294	.242	.199	.164	.135	.112	.093	.077	.064	.053	21
22	.803	.647	.522	.422	.342	.278	.226	.184	.150	.123	.101	.083	.068	.056	.046	22
23	.795	.634	.507	.406	.326	.262	.211	.170	.138	.112	.091	.074	.060	.049	.040	23
24	.788	.622	.492	.390	.310	.247	.197	.158	.126	.102	.082	.066	.053	.043	.035	24
25	.780	.610	.478	.375	.295	.233	.184	.146	.116	.092	.074	.059	.047	.038	.030	25
30	.742	.552	.412	.308	.231	.174	.131	.099	.075	.057	.044	.033	.026	.020	.015	30
40	.672	.453	.307	.208	.142	.097	.067	.046	.032	.022	.015	.011	.008	.005	.004	40
50	.608	.372	.228	.141	.087	.054	.034	.021	.013	.009	.005	.003	.002	.001	.001	50

Years Hence	16%	18%	20%	22%	24%	25%	26%	28%	30%	35%	40%	45%	50%	55%	60%	Years Hence
1	.862	.847	.833	.820	.806	.800	.794	.781	.769	.741	.714	.690	.667	.645	.625	1
2	.743	.718	.694	.672	.650	.640	.630	.610	.592	.549	.510	.476	.444	.416	.391	2
3	.641	.609	.579	.551	.524	.512	.500	.477	.455	.406	.364	.328	.296	.269	.244	3
4	.552	.516	.482	.451	.423	.410	.397	.373	.350	.301	.260	.226	.198	.173	.153	4
5	.476	.437	.402	.370	.341	.328	.315	.291	.269	.223	.186	.156	.132	.112	.095	5
6	.410	.370	.335	.303	.275	.262	.250	.227	.207	.165	.133	.108	.088	.072	.060	6
7	.354	.314	.279	.249	.222	.210	.198	.178	.159	.122	.095	.074	.059	.047	.037	7
8	.305	.266	.233	.204	.179	.168	.157	.139	.123	.091	.068	.051	.039	.030	.023	8
9	.263	.225	.194	.167	.144	.134	.125	.108	.094	.067	.048	.035	.026	.019	.015	9
10	.227	.191	.162	.137	.116	.107	.099	.085	.073	.050	.035	.024	.017	.012	.009	10
11	.195	.162	.135	.112	.094	.086	.079	.066	.056	.037	.025	.017	.012	.008	.006	11
12	.168	.137	.112	.092	.076	.069	.062	.052	.043	.027	.018	.012	.008	.005	.004	12
13	.145	.116	.093	.075	.061	.055	.050	.040	.033	.020	.013	.008	.005	.003	.002	13
14	.125	.099	.078	.062	.049	.044	.039	.032	.025	.015	.009	.006	.003	.002	.001	14
15	.108	.084	.065	.051	.040	.035	.031	.025	.020	.011	.006	.004	.002	.001	.001	15
16	.093	.071	.054	.042	.032	.028	.025	.019	.015	.008	.005	.003	.002	.001	.001	16
17	.080	.060	.045	.034	.026	.023	.020	.015	.012	.006	.003	.002	.001	.001		17
18	.069	.051	.038	.028	.021	.018	.016	.012	.009	.005	.002	.001	.001			18
19	.060	.043	.031	.023	.017	.014	.012	.009	.007	.003	.002	.001				19
20	.051	.037	.026	.019	.014	.012	.010	.007	.005	.002	.001	.001				20
21	.044	.031	.022	.015	.011	.009	.008	.006	.004	.002	.001					21
22	.038	.026	.018	.013	.009	.007	.006	.004	.003	.001	.001					22
23	.033	.022	.015	.010	.007	.006	.005	.003	.002	.001						23
24	.028	.019	.013	.008	.006	.005	.004	.003	.002	.001						24
25	.024	.016	.010	.007	.005	.004	.003	.002	.001	.001						25
30	.012	.007	.004	.003	.002	.001	.001	.001								30
40	.003	.001	.001													40
50	.001															50

The Interest Tables are reproduced by kind permission of the Australian Society of Accountants

INTEREST TABLE B

PRESENT VALUE OF £1 RECEIVED ANNUALLY FOR "n" YEARS

(Assuming that the £1 is received in a single payment on the last day of the year)

Years Hence	1%	2%	3%	4%	5%	6%	7%	8%	9%	10%	11%	12%	13%	14%	15%	Years Hence
1	.990	.980	.971	.962	.952	.943	.935	.926	.917	.909	.901	.893	.885	.877	.870	1
2	1.970	1.942	1.913	1.886	1.859	1.833	1.808	1.783	1.759	1.736	1.713	1.690	1.668	1.647	1.626	2
3	2.941	2.884	2.829	2.775	2.723	2.673	2.624	2.577	2.531	2.487	2.444	2.402	2.361	2.322	2.283	3
4	3.902	3.808	3.717	3.630	3.546	3.465	3.387	3.312	3.240	3.170	3.102	3.037	2.974	2.914	2.855	4
5	4.853	4.713	4.580	4.452	4.329	4.212	4.100	3.993	3.890	3.791	3.696	3.605	3.517	3.433	3.352	5
6	5.795	5.601	5.417	5.242	5.076	4.917	4.767	4.623	4.486	4.355	4.231	4.111	3.998	3.889	3.784	6
7	6.728	6.472	6.230	6.002	5.786	5.582	5.389	5.206	5.033	4.868	4.712	4.564	4.423	4.288	4.160	7
8	7.652	7.325	7.020	6.733	6.463	6.210	5.971	5.747	5.535	5.335	5.146	4.968	4.799	4.639	4.487	8
9	8.566	8.162	7.786	7.435	7.108	6.802	6.515	6.247	5.995	5.759	5.537	5.328	5.132	4.946	4.772	9
10	9.471	8.983	8.530	8.111	7.722	7.360	7.024	6.710	6.418	6.145	5.889	5.650	5.426	5.216	5.019	10
11	10.368	9.787	9.253	8.760	8.306	7.887	7.499	7.139	6.805	6.495	6.207	5.938	5.687	5.453	5.234	11
12	11.255	10.575	9.954	9.385	8.863	8.384	7.943	7.536	7.161	6.814	6.492	6.194	5.918	5.660	5.421	12
13	12.134	11.348	10.635	9.986	9.394	8.853	8.358	7.904	7.487	7.103	6.750	6.424	6.122	5.842	5.583	13
14	13.004	12.106	11.296	10.563	9.899	9.295	8.745	8.244	7.786	7.367	6.982	6.628	6.302	6.002	5.724	14
15	13.865	12.849	11.938	11.118	10.380	9.712	9.108	8.559	8.061	7.606	7.191	6.811	6.462	6.142	5.847	15
16	14.718	13.578	12.561	11.652	10.838	10.106	9.447	8.851	8.313	7.824	7.379	6.974	6.604	6.265	5.954	16
17	15.562	14.292	13.166	12.166	11.274	10.477	9.763	9.122	8.544	8.022	7.549	7.120	6.729	6.373	6.047	17
18	16.398	14.992	13.754	12.659	11.690	10.828	10.059	9.372	8.756	8.201	7.702	7.250	6.840	6.467	6.128	18
19	17.226	15.678	14.324	13.134	12.085	11.158	10.336	9.604	8.950	8.365	7.839	7.366	6.938	6.550	6.198	19
20	18.046	16.351	14.877	13.590	12.462	11.470	10.594	9.818	9.129	8.514	7.963	7.469	7.025	6.623	6.259	20
21	18.857	17.011	15.415	14.029	12.821	11.764	10.836	10.017	9.292	8.649	8.075	7.562	7.102	6.687	6.312	21
22	19.660	17.658	15.937	14.451	13.163	12.042	11.061	10.201	9.442	8.772	8.176	7.645	7.170	6.743	6.359	22
23	20.456	18.292	16.444	14.857	13.489	12.303	11.272	10.371	9.580	8.883	8.266	7.718	7.230	6.792	6.399	23
24	21.243	18.914	16.936	15.247	13.799	12.550	11.469	10.529	9.707	8.985	8.348	7.784	7.283	6.835	6.434	24
25	22.023	19.523	17.413	15.622	14.094	12.783	11.654	10.675	9.823	9.077	8.422	7.843	7.330	6.873	6.464	25
30	25.808	22.396	19.600	17.292	15.372	13.765	12.409	11.258	10.274	9.427	8.694	8.055	7.496	7.003	6.566	30
40	32.835	27.355	23.115	19.793	17.159	15.046	13.332	11.925	10.757	9.779	8.951	8.244	7.634	7.105	6.642	40
50	39.196	31.424	25.730	21.482	18.256	15.762	13.801	12.233	10.962	9.915	9.042	8.304	7.675	7.133	6.661	50

Years Hence	16%	18%	20%	22%	24%	25%	26%	28%	30%	35%	40%	45%	50%	55%	60%	Years Hence
1	.862	.847	.833	.820	.806	.800	.794	.781	.769	.741	.714	.690	.667	.645	.625	1
2	1.605	1.566	1.528	1.492	1.457	1.440	1.424	1.392	1.361	1.289	1.224	1.165	1.111	1.061	1.016	2
3	2.246	2.174	2.106	2.042	1.981	1.952	1.923	1.868	1.816	1.696	1.589	1.493	1.407	1.330	1.260	3
4	2.798	2.690	2.589	2.494	2.404	2.362	2.320	2.241	2.166	1.997	1.849	1.720	1.605	1.503	1.412	4
5	3.274	3.127	2.991	2.864	2.745	2.689	2.635	2.532	2.436	2.220	2.035	1.876	1.737	1.615	1.508	5
6	3.685	3.498	3.326	3.167	3.020	2.951	2.885	2.759	2.643	2.385	2.168	1.983	1.824	1.687	1.567	6
7	4.039	3.812	3.605	3.416	3.242	3.161	3.083	2.937	2.802	2.508	2.263	2.057	1.883	1.734	1.605	7
8	4.344	4.078	3.837	3.619	3.421	3.329	3.241	3.076	2.925	2.598	2.331	2.109	1.922	1.764	1.628	8
9	4.607	4.303	4.031	3.786	3.566	3.463	3.366	3.184	3.019	2.665	2.379	2.144	1.948	1.783	1.642	9
10	4.833	4.494	4.192	3.923	3.682	3.571	3.465	3.269	3.092	2.715	2.414	2.168	1.965	1.795	1.652	10
11	5.029	4.656	4.327	4.035	3.776	3.656	3.543	3.335	3.147	2.752	2.438	2.185	1.977	1.804	1.657	11
12	5.197	4.793	4.439	4.127	3.851	3.725	3.606	3.387	3.190	2.779	2.456	2.196	1.985	1.809	1.661	12
13	5.342	4.910	4.533	4.203	3.912	3.780	3.656	3.427	3.223	2.799	2.469	2.204	1.990	1.812	1.663	13
14	5.468	5.008	4.611	4.265	3.962	3.824	3.695	3.459	3.249	2.814	2.478	2.210	1.993	1.814	1.664	14
15	5.575	5.092	4.675	4.315	4.001	3.859	3.726	3.483	3.268	2.825	2.484	2.214	1.995	1.816	1.665	15
16	5.668	5.162	4.730	4.357	4.033	3.887	3.751	3.503	3.283	2.834	2.489	2.216	1.997	1.817	1.666	16
17	5.749	5.222	4.775	4.391	4.059	3.910	3.771	3.518	3.295	2.840	2.492	2.218	1.998	1.817	1.666	17
18	5.818	5.273	4.812	4.419	4.080	3.928	3.786	3.529	3.304	2.844	2.494	2.219	1.999	1.818	1.666	18
19	5.877	5.316	4.843	4.442	4.097	3.942	3.799	3.539	3.311	2.848	2.496	2.220	1.999	1.818	1.666	19
20	5.929	5.353	4.870	4.460	4.110	3.954	3.808	3.546	3.316	2.850	2.497	2.221	1.999	1.818	1.667	20
21	5.973	5.384	4.891	4.476	4.121	3.963	3.816	3.551	3.320	2.852	2.498	2.221	2.000	1.818	1.667	21
22	6.011	5.410	4.909	4.488	4.130	3.970	3.822	3.556	3.323	2.853	2.498	2.222	2.000	1.818	1.667	22
23	6.044	5.432	4.925	4.499	4.137	3.976	3.827	3.559	3.325	2.854	2.499	2.222	2.000	1.818	1.667	23
24	6.073	5.451	4.937	4.507	4.143	3.981	3.831	3.562	3.327	2.855	2.499	2.222	2.000	1.818	1.667	24
25	6.097	5.467	4.948	4.514	4.147	3.985	3.834	3.564	3.329	2.856	2.499	2.222	2.000	1.818	1.667	25
30	6.177	5.517	4.979	4.534	4.160	3.995	3.842	3.569	3.332	2.857	2.500	2.222	2.000	1.818	1.667	30
40	6.233	5.548	4.997	4.544	4.166	3.999	3.846	3.571	3.333	2.857	2.500	2.222	2.000	1.818	1.667	40
50	6.246	5.554	4.999	4.545	4.167	4.000	3.846	3.571	3.333	2.857	2.500	2.222	2.000	1.818	1.667	50